WILD FLOWER PLANT SPIRITS

BUDDHA
BEAR

# WILD FLOWER PLANT SPIRITS

## DEBRA KAATZ

### ILLUSTRATED BY

### ISIS OLIVIER

THE PETITE BERGERIE PRESS

Wild Flower Plant Spirits is published by
The Petite Bergerie Press
Les Horts, 30460, Soudorgues, France
and 27 Ondine Road, London SE15 4ED

Please consult a herbalist before taking or using any plants medicinally as the information contained in this book is not for self treatment.

*Printed in England*

Wild Flower Plant Spirits: Debra Kaatz

ISBN 0-9549166-0-3

1. Medicinal plants
2. Mind Body Spirit

Designed and typeset in Garamond by Debra Kaatz
Printed on Five Seasons recycled paper
by MPG Books Ltd, Bodmin, Cornwall
www.mpg-books.com

# CONTENTS

## A Thank You

To my parents who created me.
To my grandmother who showed me the wonders of lilac.

To all my friends and neighbours who kept asking how the book was
progressing at times when it was difficult to fire my imagination.

To all the wonderful plants of the region who each day
showed me another splendour.

To Kabir and Camille Helminski for their translations of
the poetry of Rumi and its constant inspirations.

# FOREWORD

Some years ago I was sitting in London staring at a bank of roadside 'weeds'. Hot and sunny, I lay there noting the different species of medicinal plants, my eyes chancing on a near-by clump of common mallow and mugwort, flourishing together. The sunlight picked out the delicate pinks and purples of the mallow flowers as soft and soothing in appearance as they are when applied to the skin for their emollient properties. Adrift from the world rushing by, my eyes moved on to the contrasting grey-green leaves and insignificant yellowish flowers of the mugwort, until suddenly I became aware that while I was staring at the mugwort, I was in turn being watched by an old man who had stopped beside me. I looked up, part of me hoping that he would just leave me undisturbed, but he smiled and stared straight at me with a quizzical expression.

'You look so happy!' he said, as if it was unusual to see people happy. 'I'm just looking at the flowers' I said, smiling at him. 'Yes . . . isn't it wonderful to be at one with creation again?' he replied, and with nothing else to say, shuffled slowly off down the road.

I doubt if anyone could sum up better than he did, what it feels like to lose oneself in the beauty of wild flowers. Wild flowers, far more than their cultivated cousins, beckon to us, draw us back into a world that is almost as old as the hills—a world where fact, myth and magic are alive and intertwined, and the suffering and uncertainty of our every day lives is left behind. This world is a profoundly healing place, and each wild plant has its own contribution to make to the healing that can take place here.

With its clarity—rooted in a deep understanding of the cyclical aspects of nature—and its gentle poetry, Debra Kaatz's book makes a delightful introduction to this world, giving the reader a sense of the unique properties and healing energy of some of the most beautiful and useful European medicinal plants.

To read that 'the spirit of violet is like a tiny precious gem from which comes the joy, the hope and the purpose of life within each of us,' or that 'Cherry brings a great celebration of spring to the garden and inspires the poetic heart we have inside,' reminds me of the meaning within William

Blake's much quoted lines:

'to see a world in a grain of sand and heaven in a wild flower'.

*Wild Flower Plant Spirits* will not take you to this 'heaven', because we all have to make our way there in our own special way; but whether dipped into or read from cover to cover, it will help you along the path!

Andrew Chevallier
Norfolk, 2004

'You understand that there are certain things
one should not talk about,
things that must remain hidden. If all was told . . .
then there would be no mysteries left,
and that would be very bad.
Man cannot live without mystery,
he has a great need of it.'

John Fire Lame Deer


'The word is like the nest,
the meaning is the bird,
the body is the riverbed,
and spirit, the rolling water.'

Mevlana Jelaluddin Rumi

# INTRODUCTION

Flowers open our eyes with wonder, enchant our hearts and have been given as offerings of sacred love for centuries. Each spring they bring alive the world with their promise of new life in the most vibrant colours and with the most fragrant perfumes. As the wild plum trees fill the senses with sudden hope in clouds of white blossoms, the more hidden violets bring delighted smiles to passing faces. The sun returns and warms the frozen earth into life and this sunlight is greeted by a rainbow of colours and the scents of earthly flowers. The violets in the shape of blue butterflies open their petals like wings in flight. The light powder-blue faces of a hundred speedwells follow the course of the sun throughout the day in vibrant devotion. Catkins abound on bare tree limbs tempting hungry insects. It is with explosive suddenness that the wild plum trees are filled with clouds of blossoms while everywhere else is but bare limbs.

Once the weather warms, there is no end to the exuberance of opening flowers. Where there were a handful of celandine yesterday, today there are dozens more. The cherry tree shows a few timid blossoms one day and the next day the whole tree is ablaze. It is as though the bare limbs of the earth have suddenly warmed into expressions of joy and hope. Even in cities the delicate crocuses and daffodils in the parks irresistibly charm the most hurried passerby into slowing down and breathing the spring air with a sigh of delight.

It is as though life has been inspired afresh. Deep blue violets lounge on beds of dark green leaves. The lacy flowers of shepherd's purse stand in straight lines anchored to feathered leaves near the ground. Buttery yellow daffodils shout their presence and wave their waxen spiky leaves. The small abundant sky-blue flowers of rosemary are filled with bees. The dandelion is like a powder puff covering the coats of insects with yellow pollen. No where is untouched by this miracle of spring.

Flowers brighten windows, honour sacred moments, adorn rituals and are great offerings of love and companionship. What heart does not lighten to see a field full of May poppies, or the fairy rings of crocuses around an ancient oak or all the smiles on the faces of a field of sunflowers. Have you ever pulled a petal from a clover flower and tasted its tip full of nectar? Bees gather this sweetness and at the same time pollinate each tree and flower at its most optimum time to guarantee its regeneration. Nature has spent centuries creating this precise perfection of balance and harmony. However man with his pollutions of insecticides and fertilizers, in trying to control nature, often destroys centuries of such balance. It is a fact of nature, that if we destroy insects, and bees in particular, there will be no spring flowers. But if we learn to honour and respect the earth's amazing offerings, then we will become more balanced and enriched by the beauty that surrounds us.

To go into a garden in spring, or to walk through the forest or across fields of wild flowers brings life back into the spirit. Plants have been used for centuries to heal the mind, body and the spirit. Gardens have been created to nourish the soul with beauty and harmony. The lush gardens of Granada flow with pools that are surrounded by flowers and trees that provide fragrant cool shade in the heat of the Spanish summer. The inner courtyards of the palaces of ancient emperors were filled with rare and vibrant trees and exotic plants. In the centre stands a tower where the emperor would go at times during the year to be at one with the Gods of heaven. By honouring the ancient ones the Emperor would hope to use their wisdom to bring harmony to his kingdom for the next year. The Chelsea Physic Garden in London comes from a long tradition of medicinal gardens dating from the times of the ancient Egyptian temple gardens. Such gardens were recreated in monasteries to both provide quiet places of contemplation as well to grow the medicinal herbs used for healing. Plants give us food, shelter, medicine, and beauty that fill our senses with inspiration. Even in deserts there are wonderful spring flowers after the rare rain storms. Here the oases, in the midst of vast sand oceans, are full of date trees and other greenery.

The Greeks had a myth for the creation of many plants. It was the blood of Adonis that brought forth the anemones in the spring. It was at this time that Adonis himself would come back from the dead to love Venus again. Hera was given a golden apple tree as a wedding gift by the mother earth Goddess Gaia. A nymph called Daphne turned herself into a laurel tree to escape the loving advances of Apollo. Leuce became a poplar tree. Myrrha having seduced her own father by the bewitchment of Aphrodite, in shame, turned herself into a tree. Philemon and Baucis having given Zeus food and shelter were turned into an oak and a linden tree after their death so they would never be parted. The Yew tree often lives over a thousand years and is said to gather the thoughts of the dead and then to give these thoughts to the winds to fly where they are needed. It is one of the trees that survived the Ice Age. The Indians of Mexico talk of the wind tree that is said to have great healing powers. It is from within the spirit of plants and their living essence that our understanding of their healing powers come.

In the west we can understand using the physical plant or its extracts for medicine, but the use of plants was much more than this in ancient times. In China plants were picked for a person at a certain time that was right for both the plant as well as the person in order to change what had become imbalanced. It is this untouchable realm that we experience when we are in contemplation with nature. It is a true sense of being a part of the whole energy that surrounds us and where every movement affects everything else.

Healing comes from nature. Doctors often say that if you leave the cold to heal itself it will go in a week but if he gives you something to take, the cold will go in seven days. In ancient times, as in many places today, the healer knows not only the plants but their spirits. This spirit may inspire the healer to know what plant to use and how to use it, including when to pick it. The healer knows that the plant is protected by a spirit that endows it with medicinal properties. Offerings are therefore given to this spirit when the plant is picked, so the plant will give its healing. Herbs may be used with charms and chants or in ceremonies that contact the ancient ancestors or gods to help with the negativity or disease that has infected or invaded the person. When searching for new medicines in the rainforest, plants are collected that have been shown to give results with a local healer, but when brought back to Europe have no special qualities. Indian Ayurvedic healing stresses that the plants need to be collected in the right way, at the right season, from the right soil and with the right purity of mind. For centuries the Chinese have used plants to balance the energy of the person. These were also traditionally gathered at the right time for the person. In the ancient healing world, dreams were often used as well as inner visions to help heal the person. Indeed in Greek times healing was done by having the person spend the night in a special place where healing dreams would come.

Andrew Chevallier, an English herbalist, says that 'from the earliest times, herbs have been prized for their pain-relieving and healing abilities.

Over the centuries, societies around the world have developed their own traditions to make sense of medicinal plants and their uses. Some of these traditions may seem strange and magical, others rational and sensible, but all of them are attempts to overcome illness and suffering, and to enhance the quality of life'. He goes on to say that the value of a medicinal herb cannot be reduced simply to a list of its active ingredients. Frequently, we simply do not know in detail how a particular herb works, even though its medicinal benefit is well established. For example both tea and coffee contain caffeine. However the tannins in tea reduce the amount of nutrients and drugs that are absorbed from the intestines into the blood stream which means less caffeine is absorbed than with coffee. Even at this basic level there is still a mystery of how plants work to heal.

Edward Bach in creating his flower remedies went to the plants themselves to find out how they could heal. He then said, 'Take no notice of the disease; think only of the outlook on life of the one in distress. Final and complete healing will come from the Soul itself.' He formulated the notion of personality types at a dinner party where he recognized the different gestures and behaviour of the people who surrounded him. To him it seemed there were types or families of people related emotionally by their common fears, irritability, indecision or aloofness. He felt that illness began with emotional rather than physical problems and went searching for the plants that would be equivalent to these personality types. For Bach there are various different plants that reflect the variety of soul types. These soul types he felt had the opportunity to develop through soul lessons in their life on earth. It was the flowering plant that could return a person to balance and help with the person's development. For example, with the right essence he felt that out of restraint could come love, or out of restlessness could come peace. These plants he called the twelve healers.

Eliot Cowan a healer with plant spirit medicine and a shaman tells the story of his friend who visits the native people of the Amazon. This friend is shown some plants of healing on the walk and asks how the plants are prepared and used. The whole family laughs. He is told, 'If you want to actually use a plant, the spirit of the plant must come to you in dreams.' As Eliot says, 'There is only one active ingredient in plant medicines and that is friendship. A plant spirit heals a patient as a favour to its friend-in-dreaming, the healer.' It is the case that both man and nature have spirit and in all cultures there are people who are sensitive to these spirits of nature. These are called healers or shamans who make friends with the spirits of plants and call on them for help with healing. It is this spirit of the plants that is a very strong medicine that can heal the deepest reaches of the heart and soul.

Plants speak in many different ways to each of us. Simply walking in nature often brings a deeper sense of well being if we allow our senses to be refreshed by the green wonders that surround us. Going a bit further, if you stop and rest with a tree or a plant and spend some time simply being with it and observing it, something about its character usually reveals itself. Taking this even further involves journeying. Simply lie still and close your eyes and internally journey to the spirit of the plant. When you can see the plant in your mind's eye then you can ask it about its healing qualities. This gives an even a richer understanding of the plant. For some people the plants give beautiful pictures of their spirit characters. Other people may have amazing imaginary journeys with the plants. To some people the plants inspire a new dance and others hear music. Plants are our friend, so it is important to never forget to give an offering to the plant and thank it for its help. Then you will be able to go back to the plant and enlist its help when it is needed.

This book is about the amazing beauty and potential of the wild flowers of southern France. The region is full of naturally growing wild herbs. Each flower has its own special healing quality that are still used today especially in herb teas. Hopefully by opening some of these doorways many people will be inspired to journey further into the magical world around us.

Calligraphy by Harrison Tu

# THE FIVE ELEMENTS

The Chinese say that there are five elements in nature and in turn these relate to the five seasons. For the Chinese there is spring, summer, late summer or the harvest season, autumn and winter. These also relate to the Chinese acupuncture meridians that are used to balance the Chi energy in a patient. Chi is the energy of life and the Chinese believe this energy circulates through the body in the various meridians. The state of each of these meridians is felt on the pulses. Using the five elements in acupuncture assesses the original imbalance of energy. This original imbalance relates to one of six paired meridians or one of the elements. When that balance is supported, the subsequent imbalances that occurred afterwards are also brought back into harmony. If we are in balance and live our life in harmony with the seasons then the Chinese say we will live a healthy happy life.

In ancient times a Chinese Doctor was paid for keeping a person well but if a person became ill then the Chinese Doctor was responsible for looking after the patient and his family until he was better. When we are in harmony with nature, then we can feel the burst of vitality and see with fresh hope and vision in the springtime. We will feel the joy and laughter that summer brings. We can sense the stability of a good harvest. In autumn, just as the trees loose their leaves, so we too can let go of the old unused parts of our lives to make way for the new growth in spring. In winter with the shorter days we can draw in by the fire and use the quiet of the year to harvest our inner vision in meditation.

If there is frost in the spring, then the harvest will not be as abundant and there will be less reserves for winter. In the same way when we are not balanced, our energy will find it harder to do what it needs to and our spirit may be clouded over. Bringing ourselves into contact with the spirits of plants helps us to be more aware of the imbalances within ourselves. The use of wild growing local plants can help us regain the natural harmony within ourselves. Healers, shamans, herbalist and others have healed in this way for centuries. By simply being more aware of the special qualities of the plants around us, we too can enrich our lives in ways that will help bring about more peace and harmony.

The spring brings the earth to life with an exuberance of energy. Each tree suddenly flowers and the leaves burst into life after months of wintery bare limbs. For the Chinese spring represents the season of wood and its ability to grow and prosper. The crocuses push forward and burst into flower even if it snows the next day. The insects return and fill the air with activity. Everywhere is growing and everyday a new flower appears. As one blossom appears it seems to fire the dozens of flowers that will appear the day after. There is a vitality and thrust of energy that happens at no other time in the year. Each seed comes into life and within each seed is a plan of what that life will be and how it can be put into action. Some seeds will land in rich soil and others will have to struggle to survive, but within the seed is the determination and plan of direction along with the flexibility to change and modify its growth depending on what circumstances bring. It is in spring that this urge to regenerate what we are comes again. We are given the opportunity to re-blossom like the trees around us. When this element is out of balance there may be no sense of direction or the inability to make decisions. Without a sense of direction growth will lose its sense of purpose. But with the hope and vibrancy of clear vision the spring within every one of us can blossom with the unstoppable exuberance that spring growth brings to all of nature.

In the days that follow the gardens are transformed into a great and satisfying fullness. Vegetables ripen, roses are in full bloom, and life is full of sunshine and warmth. This is summer which is the element of fire. Here is the fullness of the sun's maximum warmth that matures what the spring has brought into being. It is the warmth and love that we have within ourselves. It is the season when, with the longer hours, we have time to sit outside on the garden terrace and enjoy companionship and conversations. Life is easier and full of fresh fruits of the vine. When we have very little fire inside, we cannot share the love that naturally flows in our daily encounters. Our gateways become closed and the love from ourselves for others is sometimes no longer there. There is jealousy, or envy. One minute we are warm and then the next moment cold in our relationships. But when we can sit in the abundant gardens of summer full of roses and sunshine the most magnificent conversations can take place and warmth, enjoyment, laughter and love can flow easily. Just as plants need this extra sunshine to mature we also need this warmth from the heart to grow in our relationships.

In late summer suddenly everything ripens. The fields become golden and the apples and grapes hang heavily on the limbs of trees and vines. The flowers that were so colourful a few weeks ago are now dried seed heads. This is the season of late summer and the element of earth. It is the earth that nourishes all life without exception. She gives the best she has even when there is very little to offer, and gives in great abundance when the conditions are good. It is in this season we see the fruits of our labours and have the security of knowing that there will be enough to eat during the winter. It is a time to fill the pantry with the reserves and preserves and to see that the granaries are full for the colder days to come. This gives great stability and security to get through the winter months. Here is our mother earth who not only nourishes us but also gives us life and the earth beneath our feet on which to stand. We are her children and when we are out of balance we cannot feel the security and warmth that babies feel in their mother's arms. We lose our sense of centre and have no ground to stand on. But when our harvest is full, we again have this sense of the security of being in the very lap of mother nature herself. In this way we can give to everyone else what they need with the same generosity that the earth gives to us.

The days soon grow colder and shorter and suddenly the world is filled with all the green leaves of summer turning the most vividly bright reds, yellows and browns. Soon all growth of the summer that has not been harvested will fall to the ground and enrich the soil for the next year. It is dramatic in the fall how, when the leaves fall away, there is suddenly so much light where there was shade before. It is as though the heavenly light and clarity return with the crystal sharpness of the autumn air. This is the element of metal. It is a time when the precious nutrients fall into the ground to nourish the next year. We too need a time when the old growth and dead leaves can fall back into the soil so new growth can come in the spring. The Chinese felt the element metal also related to the heavenly father. It was from the skies that came the air that gives life. It is by taking in the inspiration through the breath from the air around us and by exhaling and letting go of the unusable rubbish, that each moment is transformed and each step is taken along the pathway of the Tao. Without this ability to let go we would soon be filled with rubbish, but by letting go we are then able to take in the inspirations that the heavens offer us in each moment. Here we can find the quality and specialness in what life offers.

The days soon grow shorter and the landscape becomes bare as the winter winds bring storms and snows. All the seeds of late summer lie deep within the earth, sleeping. The Chinese felt one should follow the seasons and in winter it was wise to nourish one's reserves. It is a time to sit by the fire and keep warm and meditate in the quietness that is winter. The landscape itself is silent and empty with only the bare limbs of trees showing. But the reserves of water are replenishing the reservoirs that will provide the much needed water for summer. The element of winter is water with its great reserves and depths. Winter requires survival and we have to draw on what has been stored the rest of the year in order to live through the colder months. Nothing can stop water when it floods out of control and when there is a drought nothing can stop the fear that everything may die. When the water element within us is balanced it gives us our greatest reserves and the determination to survive no matter what hardships confront us.

All of us have each of these five elements within, bringing balance and harmony to our body, minds and spirits. When we become out of balance, the spirit of nature herself helps to put things back into equilibrium again. Every wild flower has its own special ability to help heal in this way through its spirit. We get a sense of this walking through a forest where we feel more refreshed and alive and can feel the natural changes of each season. The descriptions of the following flowering plants is just the beginning to opening many doors into not only a healing world but the richly creative world of spirit itself. The interpretations are my own and are there to inspire interest and curiosity. Everyone's experience will be different. These tastes and experiences of the richness of wild flowers, will hopefully stimulate some of you to go further into making even deeper contact with the natural wildernesses within yourselves that will honour, protect and save the world around us.

This world of spirit is all around us. When we enter a garden in the summer there is something very special that opens our senses. It is amazing how each plant and blade of grass grows together in harmony. The same happens in a forest where every tree grows alongside every other tree creating a vast space of cathedral green bringing a quiet contemplation to all around it. Here in this calming peace of beauty we are given a sense of the spirit of the wholeness of all things living together, each affecting the other. Trees have been on the earth for centuries, long before man was even a thought. The seeds of all those trees have produced one generation after another Within each tree lies every other tree that has gone before it and in its seed contains every tree that will follow. Life in this way is continuous and completely interdependent.

Each living thing has a purpose and a beauty that blossoms forth like a fragrant flower on a summer's day. When we look into a baby's eyes we can see the life, vitality and fascination for life. Every thing is new and exciting. The Chinese say that we can only know things with our hearts, for those things worth knowing are about the spirit of ourselves and every thing around us. When we are distracted by everyday life we loose this ability to see what is around us, what gives us love, peace and harmony. We lose the open curiosity of a young child. By entering the garden, the forest or the park, we enter a place where the natural world is full of its own spirit and it naturally brings us back into harmony with ourselves, awakening our own spirit.

When we contact the world of plant spirits we are going further into this contemplation. In a sense, by natural evolution, we were all plants at one time before they developed into insects, animals and then people. We have within us this connection to both the plant and its ability to heal. By lying still in nature and going into this calm quiet space we can again make contact with the spirit and very essence of each wild flowering plant around us. It is then that our heart and spirit can hear and see with inner ears and eyes the beautiful spirit of each plant. By making this direct contact, the plants themselves reveal their inner nature by giving us images of who they are. We can then enter into conversations in which they can be asked for their help, healing and any other knowledge that maybe helpful. It is also true that when we return from this reverie, the plants themselves take on a new life and we are able to sense and feel more as we wander in the natural world around us.

# WILD FLOWER PLANT SPIRITS

# VIOLET
## *Viola*

The violet is a flower that is desirable for its sweet scent. It has the rare quality of suddenly appearing in the most unusual places. Its flower has petals that seem to shyly smile on an abundant bed of richly dark green leaves like a rare violet butterfly about to take flight. These flowers open in undistinguished corners and make those corners suddenly magical. The violets are one of the first flowers to appear in the spring, tempting the eye with their colour, the nose with their sweet fragrance, and the spirit with their delicacy. The violet never interferes with other plants and happily hides in long grasses or in the cracks of old stone walls. It is always distinctly on its own and is a very precious treasure of the garden with a calmness of purpose. It announces the spring with a quiet surprise.

In Greek mythology, Zeus was always falling in love. This particular time it was with the beautiful nymph Io. In order to keep Hera, his wife, from knowing, he turned Io into a beautiful calf and asked the earth to create a fragrant flower for the calf to eat. The earth brought forth a field of violets. Hera seeing this beautiful calf with violets in her mouth was not convinced it was just any calf and sent a gadfly to bite it. Io ran into the sea to avoid the gadfly. Zeus confessed and Hera made him promise not to look at Io again. When he gave his promise, Io was changed back into a nymph. The violet has remained in meadows ever since.

The violet is associated with another myth. Orpheus was born a poet and it is said that honeyed words flowed from his lips. He was famous for his songs and lute playing. When his wife died, he descended into the underworld and charmed Hades with his singing and eloquence. His wife was allowed to return provided she did not look back until she entered the world again. Just at the threshold she forgot, looked back and had to return. When Orpheus died his lute fell to the ground and on that spot the first violets were said to bloom. Zeus then took the lute and placed it among the stars.

Violets have been used in sacred rites and festivities for centuries. The Greeks made them into garlands for the hair, and perfumes to sweeten the senses and clear the head. They saw the violet as a symbol of fertility. It was a flower that was sacred to Aphrodite, the goddess of love. It was often added to love potions or was used to decorate love tokens and treasure boxes. Ancient Greeks wore violets to calm tempers and to induce sleep. In medieval times violet wine, cordials and jellies were made. It was said that wearing a crown of violets on the head would cure a headache and carrying the flowers would bring good luck. It was also believed that if the leaves were worn in a green sachet it would help wounds to heal. Violets were often offered in bunches in the springtime to awaken the senses with odour and colour after the long winter. Gathering the first violet you saw in spring was said to ensure that your greatest or dearest wish would be granted. The Druids would drink violet wine on both the winter and summer solstices to bring luck, protection, peace and healing. Gerard in his herbal says that they are beautiful and graceful to behold enabling the mind to be good and honest and giving it the fragrance to inspire what is comely and honest. He says that violets bring to a liberal and gentle mind the remembrance of honesty, comeliness and all kinds of virtues. He felt one handful of violets would surpass all the pleasant flowers that grow in the world.

Violets have for centuries been mixed with medicines to comfort and strengthen the heart. According to Culpepper, they are cold and moist while being fresh and green and can be used to cool any heat or distemper of the body either inwardly or outwardly. Their leaves have been used for gout, bronchitis, sore throats, poor nerves, eczema, rheumatism, and insomnia. The flowers are often used in syrups for coughs. The root has been used for external bruises and swellings. In present day herbalism the violet flowers and root are used as an infusion or syrup for treating colds, coughs and congestion. The flowers and leaves are used in British herbalism to treat breast and stomach cancer.

Violets are gentle and happy to be by themselves. After the winter storms, they give the appearance of tranquility and beauty as they lift their sweet flowers with dignity and gracefully adorn the spring. They are a flower that brightens up dark places of shade for they know that each day will increase in light. It is the nature of the violet to sense the renewed vision of that returning light. When the violet appears we remember the years before and the springs of other violets. We sense the changes that will come with the next year. This is the violet's ability to renew and brighten everything.

The spirit of violet is like a tiny precious gem from which comes the joy, the hope and the purpose of the life within each of us. When we find this beautiful sense of purpose within, it gives an enormous sense of calm and well being. Here we can create out of the spontaneity of the moment, just as the violet surprises us with delight when it suddenly emerges from its corner. It is like the butterfly we cannot catch hold of but must allow to come to us in quietness. It then fills us with the pleasure, inspiration and vitality of what it wants to offer at that moment in time. Here is a secret place where we remember the honesty of who we are and smile sweetly in the contentment of that vision. Seen in this way the violet is indeed a very precious treasure of the garden.

Imagine a wooden box of your favourite wood. Decorate it in your imagination with what you find beautiful, flowers, shells, patterns, stars, lights, signs or anything else. Carefully select the hinges and the latch that opens the box. Does it have a key and if so what kind of key. Now examine the inside of the box. Is it engraved, does it have a material lining of old silk or linen or quilt material? Now look and see what is inside this most delightful box. Take it out and examine what it is and record it in some way. Draw it, or paint it, or write a story or invent a poem. Then simply be with the beauty of your creation and keep it in your memory. Violet were often pressed and then glued onto paper or ribbons. Imagine this treasure of yours being pressed onto precious paper to be forever kept as a keepsake. Violet enables us to touch those gems of beauty within ourselves and to then use them in the world. Here is our violet fragrance, our special face or voice delighting all around us with its own special beauty in the same way the violet adorns the garden with its charming smile.

*'Violets —*
*How precious on a mountain path.'*

Bashō

# WILLOW
## *Salix*

At the end of winter it is still cold and everywhere is bare and seems lifeless. Then suddenly one day the wonderful catkins hang like Christmas ornaments on the willow tree. Life has come again bringing with it great delight. Hope is rekindled and we know life will soon fill the empty branches. The fresh leaves of willow are the most delicate fresh light green. It is what the Chinese call the alchemical green of life. One can see the spirit of each willow tree come alive as these delicate leaves emerge. There is a lightness and grace about willow trees. It is as though they dance among other trees of the forest with an unhindered spirit that rekindles life. Just watching a willow tree with these vibrant leaves dancing in the breezes, whispering with the wind, brings our spirits alive just as the spring revitalizes the tree itself. They are the youthful child trees of the forest.

In early spring the willows are adorned with catkins giving the bees their first feast after the long winter. Their delicate light green leaves appear as the wild cherry trees flower. They are the joy and vitality of the vibrancy that is spring itself. The willow loves water and has an amazing capacity to regenerate itself. Branches can be cut back and it will repush new ones that can be cut back again the next year. Old trees fall to the ground and out of them grow up new trees. There is a story of a woman gardener being given a present wrapped in a willow branch and her sticking the branch in the ground to grow the first willow tree of that region. The branches are easily bendable and were traditionally used for making cradles, baskets, furniture, cricket bats and even harps. The trees use wind energy on their leaves to increase evaporation that then increases the amount of water and nutrients taken up by the soil.

The bark has been used for centuries to relieve joint pain and manage fevers. According to Gerard the leaves were traditionally used to staunch the bleeding of wounds. In more recent times the bark of willow was found to contain salicin which aspirin was originally made of until a synthetic substitute was found. Interestingly the bark is also used as an anti-inflammatory for arthritic and rheumatic conditions. Returning this flexibility to the body is a part of the willow's very nature. In current herbal medicine the willow is used as an excellent remedy for arthritic and rheumatic pain affecting the back, knee and hip joints. It relieves inflammation and swelling, and improves mobility in painful or creaky joints. It can be taken to manage high fever and to ease headaches and head pain. It also reduces sweating and therefore can help hot flashes and night sweats.

All willows have leaves that shimmer in the wind. The whispering leaves were often listened to as oracles or messages of the gods. The branches have been used for centuries as divining rods and for telling prophecies. They are traditionally used in consulting the I Ching and thrown to reveal the Hexagons of divination. Other soothsayers place the rods on open ground and utter their predictions as they pick up each one. In Scotland the clan chiefs would hold up a peeled willow wand when speaking justice. In Greek mythology, Persephone the queen of the underworld, had a sacred grove of aged willows to which Odysseus was sent by Circe to meet the spirit of a dead mystic who could see the future. Orpheus was said to have touched one of the willows in Persephone's grove to give him eloquence for when he passed through the underworld to bring back his wife. Poseidon, the god of the sea also had a sacred willow grove dedicated to him. The Greek word for willow is 'helice'. Mount Helicon took its name from this word for willow and was the home of the nine Muses who inspired and brought music, poetry, theatre and all aspects of culture to mankind.

In Celtic mythology there is the festival of Imbolc. This happens at winter's ending and celebrates the returning sun after the winter's darkness. At that time the goddess Brighid is said to carry a white willow wand to fertilize the land. She regenerates the lifeless land, bringing back the greenery and giving new births to animals. She is said to breathe life back into the mouth of the deadness of winter. Women would gather gifts to offer at her shrine to bring fertility, intuition and inspiration. She is the goddess of inspiration, healing and the forge where the magician smithy would transform underworld elements into objects of sacred beauty.

The willow has been decorated in festivals celebrating the springtime. Messages or pieces of material or clothes are tied to the tree to both honour its life giving spirit as well as to ask for a message. The Gypsies would celebrate the spring festival in April by cutting down a willow tree. It would be set up in the ground and decorated with leaves and garlands made of spring greenery. It was said that if a woman who was pregnant placed one of her garments under the willow tree overnight and found a leaf upon the garment the next morning then her labour would be easy. Sick people would ask it to die but to let them live. After the celebrations the tree, or a smaller version of the tree, was thrown into the river to wake up the water spirits and regenerate the growth of all things. It is said that if you wish to know if you will be married in the next year, you must find a willow tree on New Year's Eve and throw your shoe into the branches. If it sticks in the branches then you will be wed sometime in the next year. You have eight chances to succeed. The leaves, wood and bark of the willow are both used for healing as well as to bring protection. Magical brooms were traditionally bound with willow branches.

The willow has flexibility and when we have this same flexibility we can move smoothly through life. But like the willow, when life is full of old unbendable dead wood, we become irritated, angry and frustrated that others seem to have a joyful purposeful life and we cannot see what is there for us. When we can see and feel what we are meant to do and have a vision of our own purpose in life, our fear of life disappears and the joy to invite experience and adventure into our life gives us the same flexibility as the willow. It is as though we come out of the winter sleep and brightly grow into who we are. We are then able to walk our path, face our challenges and accept what comes with tolerance and flexibility. It is this visionary sense of purpose that the willow brings.

Rest with your back against a willow tree and watch how the light of the sun shimmers through the leaves and branches. This is the lightness and playfulness that awakens vision out of the shaded darkness. It is a vision full of organization, decisions, purpose, with a driving force that comes from real understanding of what can be achieved in life. The willow has this driving force that constantly renews itself each spring, creating new growth for the next year. All seeds have this same dynamic energy that allows them to burst open in the spring and grow into whatever plant they are meant to be. If this driving energy is blocked then there is frustration and even anger. If the vision of what someone or something is clouds over, then there is no hope. But when this energy to move forward is fired by the vision of what something will become, then each seed flowers fully and each life blossoms into its very essence. The spirit of willow gives us this hopeful ease and playfulness.

# WILD PLUM
## *Prunus Domestica*

Out of winter's bitter cold winds come longer days and the first flowering tree to come out of the long cold sleep is the wild plum. The Chinese call it one of the three friends of winter along with the cold resisting pine and the chill enduring bamboo. Its blossoms are like vibrant white clouds that dance amidst the barren brown landscape. In this stark contrast one can see the unstoppable energy of life when the moment is exactly right for bursting into full flower. The plum tree is suddenly alive with not just one but hundreds of blossoms filled with pure gold centres. Out of these blossoms come the fruits that will make Chinese plum sauce, plum jam, German küchen and the fiery liqueur called slivowitz. Mabey calls the wild plum one of the best wild foods. Plum varieties are extensive and in the wild they cross with other trees like the blackthorn. They alone often remain on sites of long-deserted habitations. They give great nourishment to the spirit as well as the body. When we are filled with hundreds of blossoms, we too can produce great richness.

The white blossoms are filled with gold stamens and pollen. It is as though the sun has concentrated its golden dust in the very heart of each blossom. The birds begin their songs and mating in earnest when these delicate flowers appear. Plums are very vivacious trees producing new trees either by their roots or by fallen seeds. Other fruit trees are often grafted onto the hardy roots of plums for this reason. It is the plums that are at home in the soil and environment that surrounds them. It is this whole environment that they bring to life in the spring. The plum blossoms even if it snows for it seems to know that it is time for everything to grow again. It is like the spring alarm of the seasonal clock of the garden.

The Indians of North America used wild plum branches to make prayer sticks. The branches were peeled and painted and then a feather or some tobacco was tied to the top as an offering. They were made to heal a sick person and used as offerings to the gods. Gerard says the leaves of the plum tree placed in wine are good against the swelling of the uvula (soft palate), the throat, gums and jaws. Culpepper found the dried leaves and fruit to be a diuretic and laxative. The leaves can also be used to lower fever. In the Bach remedies, wild plum essence is used for when someone is in fear of losing their mind or in dread of doing something frightful. It is used for the desperation of deep depression. Its positive aspect is seen as a calm quiet courage.

It is not by accident that the plum blossoms emerge out of winter with such vitality. Winter is a time that tests our endurance to its limits. We must draw on our reserves to protect ourselves from the cold and long nights. In ancient times the winter solstice was celebrated to honour the returning sun upon which the new harvest would depend. Stone circles and long barrows were constructed in such a way that at sunrise on the solstice the sun would illuminate the entire chamber or fall in a direct line with certain stones of the circle. In this way it was believed that the earth would be awakened for the next year and the sun would return. It is said that the buds of trees know and are sensitive to the movements of the sun, moon and stars. The buds of each tree vibrate differently and have different vibrations related to the movements of the heavens. Somehow the plum tree knows when it is time for spring and rejuvenates all around it with its full blossoms.

It has the power to regenerate itself through its own fruits that can be cross pollinated into new varieties or by its branches being grafted onto strong wild roots of the region. This was how the damsons from Byzantine came to be grafted onto roots in Europe and today are found everywhere. Plums come in all colours from sunripe yellows to greengages to deep almost black damsons. There is no limit to the plum's variations. It is this transformative quality that gives it its strength and vitality and allows it to survive. Wild plum trees grow in the most amazing places. They can be found growing out of cracks in the rock face or along walls, or in poor soil. When the circumstances are more nourishing it blossoms forth with remarkable speed and abundance.

It uses the strength of the returning sunshine, the powering force of our universe, to move out of the darkness of winter. Its blossoms fill with this fresh exuberance creating richly nutritious fruits. It is as though it harvests the light of winter and at just the right moment sets the spring into motion with clouds of energetic blossoms. It is this energy and light that at times is needed to move out of the deep depressions and desperations that can come when our spirit has endured too long or when our resources cannot cope with the dark coldness that winters our soul. At times like these, we need to feel the sun's return. We need to feel the sap once again rise in our veins and be filled with the energy that sets each bud into a flower that has the potential to become a nourishing fruit. When we are filled with this light and vision and when this energy and vision are rekindled in us, then even the most difficult circumstances can be handled with calm, quiet courage.

Imagine being cold, and contracted in a dark place without any light. It is so depressing that there is no joy in life. Then feel warm rain and sunshine bringing life back into your very bones. Really enjoy this warmth moving the very essence of your being. Feel the sap rise from your innermost centre outwards to all your limbs. Have a delight in growing in height and breadth from pure sunlight and vibrant water. Imagine like a tree you are suddenly full of fresh green leaves able to make all the nourishment you need from the sunlight, minerals in the ground, and fresh spring water. Then open your arms to the heavens and feel all the seasonal changes that are constantly flowing with the movements of the winds. Feel these changes from your very centre and watch their exquisite results. This is the awakened vision that is the spirit of the plum tree. In this way the spirit is nourished again and feels a part of all around it. With the spirit of wild plum our life regains the faith and courage to live life to its fullest.

*'I cannot see which is which:*
*the glowing plum blossom is the spring night's moon.'*

Izumi Shikibu

# LESSER CELANDINE
## *Ranunculus Ficaria*

The lesser celadine appears even before the flowering plum. It is called the messenger of spring and is said to come with the arrival of the swallows. It certainly blooms to announce their arrival as they set to work building their nests under the eaves of old stone houses. Although it grows very low on the ground, its flowers are like bright sparkling eyes that seem to have awakened with the warming sunshine. The bright yellow flowers seem to radiate this warmth with an affection all their own. The colour is especially lively and bright bringing the fields and woodlands alive with hundreds of these flowers that seem to twinkle with sunlight. This flower appears on the tombstone of Wordsworth who said of this favourite flower of his that 'the painter who first tried to picture the rising sun, must have taken the idea of the spreading pointed rays from the celandine's glittering countenance'. It is as though the sun has simply poured into this flower's very happy nature. The petals, being very sensitive, open and close with the light and temperature of the air. The Celts actually named them after the sun for this reason. The blossoms would shut if it was raining and when the sun was out would only open in the full sunlight. Lesser celadine suddenly disappears in May and is not seen again until the next year.

Its Latin name, ranunculus ficaria, is made of ranunculus which is thought to come from the Latin for frog and ficaria which means fig. It was thought that the plant liked the same habitat as the frog or a place where it was moist and dark. The fig refers to the tubers which form both on the roots as well as under the leaves. Those under the leaves become self pollinated seeds that drop into the soil in the summer.

Gerard in his herbal explains that the root mixed with wine is good for piles and the juice of the root mixed with honey purges the head. In more recent times the plant has been given the name of pilewort because it is still used for haemorrhoids. Its name comes from the Greek word, chelidon meaning swallow. In folk remedies it is said that if lesser celadine is warmed in a glass of white wine and drunk before bed, the person will be assured of pleasant dreams. In ancient times it was thrown on the fire to celebrate the return of the growing sunshine. It was believed to be a visionary herb that could be used to bathe the third eye and open vision and intuition. It has been used as a herb of protection and can impart good spirits or joy if worn.

Through the fall and winter, trees and plants shed their old dead leaves and wood. The winter storms and snows then clear away old branches and limbs of bushes and shrubs. This serves both to fertilize the soil with decay as well as to remove the old wood so the trees will put all their effort into the new growth. The old thoughts, actions, habits and beliefs have to be cleared away and let go of, before the spring can bring its brightness of renewed vision. The birds return to their northern homes and sweep out their nests from the previous spring, making clean fresh nests for the next generation.

Spring is a time when life is regenerated. It is the time when the hearth is swept clean of the wintery cinders and the windows are opened to the warm fresh air. We often talk about spring cleaning and unpacking the boxes of summer clothes and putting away the winter clothes. Trees shed their bark and grow larger with new skin at this time. Flowers push up through the nourishing compost. Insects appear out of the earth to once again gather seeds. Here we emerge out of the old year and see the promise of the next year with fresh eyes.

Celadine is not a modest or shy plant, but radiates with charm and boldly says that she is there enjoying and responding to all the changes around her. There is an honesty and determination in her brightly coloured flowers that expresses the purpose of spring as a time for each life to burst forth in its own unique way. Hers is a freshness of purpose in being simply what one is. There is this essence in all of us that gets renewed each spring and this brings the inspiration for the next year.

Lesser celadine announces the spring as a time when everything can grow afresh out of the compost of the last year. It is no wonder she seems to cover the earth with vibrantly clear yellow flowers as bright as a thousand new born eyes. Eyes eager to see the world afresh in all its splendours and potentials. Here we too can leave old habits and thoughts behind and breathe in the freshness and lightness of who we are. With our vision renewed we can move forward enriched by what has gone before and change with what now needs to come.

There was once a wood where no flowers grew. A sparrow visited the wood to make its nest. She brought yellow flowers to make the nest soft and warm and laid three eggs on this rich golden carpet. In time the three eggs hatched into little sparrows hungry for food. The mother searched high and wide for food, bringing back what she could find. The little birds grew bigger and their feathers lengthened until at last they were able to fly. In the autumn the whole family flew to a warmer shelter in the southern forest for the winter. The winter winds blew strong and hard and the nest fell to the ground. The rain washed the seeds of the yellow flowers into the ground where they were covered with old leaves until the following spring. As the weather warmed and the rains came, a single seed began to grow. At first it was a delicate shoot and then some leaves appeared and it grew stronger and stouter. Suddenly out of the cluster of rich green leaves a stem appeared and grew straight and tall. For two whole weeks it grew until at last a swelling appeared at the top. Each day the sun would shine through the leaves of the forest on the plant and one morning as the sun appeared the swelling opened into a simple yellow flower. The celandine had blossomed like a tiny golden ray of sunshine. This vibrant new shiny flower of celadine had come out of the rich old compost of the autumn. It is this flowering out of the richness of the old that celadine expresses.

*'Become earth that you may grow
flowers of many colours.'*

Mevlana Jelaluddin Rumi

# CHERRY
## *Prunus Avium*

The cherry tree in blossom in the spring awakens the poetic visions of the heart and has been the inspiration of poets all over the world. It flowers at a time when the gardens are beginning to bloom everywhere. At this point in time the cherry tree adds its elegance, making the whole garden a poetic picture. The cherry needs space to grow and is at the edge or in clearings in the wooded hillsides. It is as though it demands this creative space in order to give everything else its beauty.

Just before the cherry tree is due to burst forth, the Japanese invite their friends to come for the special day and encourage the cherry tree itself to wake up by playing drums below its branches. On the day everyone comes and celebrates the awakening of the cherry tree. Lying in a hammock under a flowering cherry tree is like being in heaven itself. The leaves adorn the hanging white flowers with golden centres and the delicate scent fills the heart with wonder and beauty. The bees celebrate its flowering by drinking its blossom nectar as a whole hive together, buzzing with sweet contentment. It is said in China that the flowering of the cherry tree transports us to the lands of the immortals. Indeed one can imagine the great spirits celebrating and drinking together under an ancient cherry tree somewhere in the heavenly gardens above.

The wild cherry grows at the edge of forests or in clearer places as it needs light for its pollination. It is a relatively short lived tree but its wood has been used for centuries to make beautiful objects. It can be polished until it is like fine mahogany. The smell of cherry wood is fragrant and delicate as is the tree itself. The fruits themselves are many different varieties varying in colour from yellow to red to even deep purple or black. They are always in bunches and eating cherries is one of the early delights from the gardens. The wild cherries are small but often used in cakes or brandies. The sticky resin that come out of the bark can be used as a kind of chewing gum. In older times branches of cherry were hung in the house to ward off fevers. The Japanese say to find love you simply tie one strand of your hair to a blossoming cherry tree. Because it is often in blossom or budding near Easter time its branches are used for decorations in the Church. It is the cherry that brings a great celebration of spring to the garden and inspires the poetic heart we have inside.

The bark of the wild cherry tree has been used medicinally. When boiled into a fusion or tea and drunk it reduces the cough reflex and eases fevers and colds. The Indians used it to ease labour pains. Cherry stems are still used for urinary problems. The cherries themselves are said to be good for arthritis. Cherries soaked in brandy after several months makes a delicious liquor that is said to bring the delights of the flowering tree back to our senses, warming our spirit and tongue with poetic verse.

The cherry is the heart, the joy and the celebration of springtime. The spirit soars lying under the clouds of blossoms each filled with pure gold. Here the palace gateways open and we are surrounded by our own elegance. Here we can dream our hopes and desires without the worldly cares that normally cloud over our vision. When cherries are served as a desert, our tastes are delighted and we don't need anything else. But to rise to even greater culinary delights we can pour flaming cherries over crepes and bathe our senses in pure elegance. In the same way, when we refind and are able to see the real purpose in our lives then we become satisfied and our needs grow less. It is then that our imagination has the space to soar. Relaxing under clouds of cherry blossoms our minds are able to fly to memories and dreams we may have long ago lost sight of or have been too busy to think about for a long time.

Here under the cherry tree we are able to imagine ourselves greater because we become a part of the beauty that the cherry tree expresses in us. We can rediscover the treasures and pleasures in simply being who we are. Then with a sigh of delight we can feel our talents rise up within us just as the sap of spring brings the cherry out of its sleep to once again dress itself in magnificent splendour. It is in this reverie that we can feel from our heart who we are and reach outwards with creative energy.

It is in this quiet, calm reverie in the beautiful place of the cherry tree that our thoughts and feelings can wander to those places we can only imagine. The heavens above us open and thoughts, ideas and images come without effort to inspire our very nature. Here in this special place of day dreams we have the ability to wander and change things and see the other side of circumstances. It is here that words form images rather than actions. Although those images maybe put into action. Here we have new ideas that seem to come from beyond. Suddenly we find a poetic phrase or picture comes on its own and inspires and enlightens our moment. By staying in this place of meditation we begin to see the beauty within the world and others. It is here that we cease to be and the world guides our thoughts and visions.

In ancient times in the great palace of the Emperor there was an inner garden. Magical animals such as the unicorn and the winged horse would visit. Water sang as it moved through the terraces forming poems in gurgling streams, visions in still pools and music in stately canals. As a young boy, the Emperor planted a flowering cherry tree in the centre of the garden. Each year when it flowered he would watch the clouds of blossoms and would see the previous year pass and watch the vision form of the next year to come. Each year, before he would leave the presence of the cherry tree, the tree would drop a beautiful blossom onto his hand. This blossom lasted for the whole of the year. The Emperor would give the tree a small present and bury it under its roots before leaving. Finally as an old man, the Emperor came again one spring bringing the tree a crystal cup of pure spring water and poured it on the trees roots. He rested under the magnificent blossoms and looked back on his life with love and peace. The gateway opened to the heavens and as his spirit passed into the next life and his body died on earth the tree lovingly took his body into its own roots. The wisdom of the Emperor was ever after heard in the winds that whispered through the branches of the cherry tree. For generations after, whoever sat beneath the cherry tree would feel the love of the Emperor in their hearts and this warmth would give their vision the most beautiful images. Anyone who came and sat with the tree became an artist in their own special way afterwards. It became the tree of artists and when it was too old to flower, the ancient gardener cut the old wood away and out of the roots came a vibrant new shoot that soon became another tree of inspiration. This inspiration is the heart of the spirit of the cherry tree.

*'Spring night, cherry-blossom dawn.'*

Bashō

# COWSLIP
## *Primula Veris*

To see cowslips in the spring is like falling in love again. They have very soft delicately green leaves out of which come the most charming lantern shaped flowers with soft yellow petals at the end. The flowers appear above the richly veined leaves like lanterns of yellow shining in all directions. Here is a posy of spring time just waiting to be caressed. They are like little bouquets splashed among the tall grasses and along old walls and pathways. One can imagine fairies coming out in full moonlight just to dance underneath their flowers. They weave a spell of enchantment in the magical way the flowers are suspended on a single delicate stalk. They express the fragile delicate life that comes into being each spring with all its fresh sensual pleasures.

Cowslip is the prima rosa or the first rose of spring. It is also called the butter rose because of its colour. It represents both the spring and first love. It is said that if young girls make the flowers into balls their thoughts would tend towards marriage. Posies are made by stringing the flowers together at their ends and tying the string tight so all the flowers stand out. Holding the flowers in their hands and closing their eyes the young maidens are said to foresee their future husband. The very first posy of cowslips in the spring had to contain thirteen flowers, if brought into the house, or the hens would lay badly. It has many associations with early youth and in ancient times represented the time when childhood matured into adulthood. In this way it was said to symbolize purity and youthfulness. Children still gather the flowers and string them together to form a cowslip ball in the spring.

Cowslip is often hidden among the tall grasses of the fields. At other times it sits in twos or threes along pathways or by old stone walls. Its flowers rise above the leaves and hang like flowering Japanese lanterns with youthful yellow flowers at the end. It is quite adventurous growing where it lands and finds space for itself even in the most overgrown places. There is an independence about its nature as well as a delicate beauty. This charm and beauty were some of the reasons that the cowslips became one of the Celtic fairy flowers that were said to grow in places where rings of enchantment could be woven.

In Celtic times the cowslip was prized as a plant that could open vision and protect the opening of that vision. The Druids would initiate bards with a drink made from cowslip and vervain. They would also rub oil mixed with the flowers into their skin as a cleanser and purifier before rituals. The flower is connected to the spring goddess and was carried for protection and to honour the springtime. Placed in front of a house it was said to discourage visitors. When carried or worn it was said to preserve youth. If you hold a bunch of cowslips flowers in your hand it is thought it will help to find a hidden treasure. It was said in ancient times it could grant access to the heavens. It was also associated with the sensual currents of the seasons and the growth of life and fertility. It is a plant that awakens the fullness of the senses and in such a way inspires life and its meaning.

The flowers have been used to make wine since ancient times and the Romans were particularly good at making a strong version. They were also used as a tea that has sedative qualities. An infusion of the roots can be useful for the gout and rheumatism. According to Culpepper the dried and powdered roots were good for nervous disorders. The roots have traditionally been used to ease the back and help urination as well as giving relief for coughs and colds. A tea or tincture of the flowers is said to relieve nightmares and nervous pain. An ointment made with the flowers helps with sunburn and is also said to take away wrinkles of the skin. The flowers have been carried by women to attract love and have long been used to help preserve beauty. The sixteenth century herbalist, William Turner wrote, that women would mix cowslip flowers with white wine to wash their faces and make them 'fair in the eyes of the world rather than the eyes of God who they were not afraid to offend'. If it is added to the bath water it is said to increase beauty. When it is planted in the garden it is said to protect the house and all around it.

In today's herbalism the cowslip root and its leaves are used for chronic coughs such as bronchitis. The root is thought to slow blood clotting. The flowers are believed to be sedative and are used for overactivity and sleeplessness. They are also antispasmodic and anti-inflammatory which could make them potentially useful for asthma and other allergic conditions.

The plant has a sweetness to it. Its leaves and flowers have a velvety softness to them. Indeed it is like a spring child that is comfortable and secure wherever it is. It is able to adjust itself and integrate itself into whatever situation it finds itself. According to tradition it can tell about love. Because it is in harmony with everything around it, love surrounds it. It is like a pool of golden sunlight that bathes the senses in loving sensuality. Here is the freshness that we all once had as children delighting in whatever pleasures came our way.

Imagine lying in a field of sunshine on the new soft grasses of early springtime. Close your eyes and listen to all the wonderful sounds surrounding you, the movement of the grass, the insects walking, the birds calling, the gusts of wind moving branches, and the gurgling of a passing stream. Then be aware of all the fragrances that are all around, the crushed grass, the leaves warmed in the sunshine, the sweetness of flowers, the perfumes on the air itself and the smell of water or rain in the air. Feel the grass patterns on your back, the softness of flower petals on your finger tips, the grass leaves on your cheeks, and the wind on your hair. Ask the cowslip for some special nourishment for your senses and spirit. Enjoy the gift that she gives. Spend some time really savouring what you receive. Thank her and give her something in return.

Then open your eyes and see all the insects move, watch the birds fly across the sky, meditate on the clouds drifting on blue infinity and refresh yourself with all the fantastic colours everywhere. Taste the poppy seeds, the fresh water of a spring, the breath of the wind and the droplets of rain. Nature constantly feeds our senses with all these wonders, filling us with the vitality of a heavenly well, and a golden sea opening our senses to the beauties all around. This nourishment and refreshment is the spirit of cowslip bringing alive our sensibilities to the world we live in and feeding us with all its pleasures.

*'There is a garden in every childhood, an enchanted place*
*where colours are brighter, the air softer,*
*and the morning more fragrant than ever again.'*

Elizabeth Lawrence

# NETTLE
## *Urtica Dioica*

The nettle is known for its sting. It has hairs along its stem and leaves that pierce the skin that cause it to burn. But it has its own cure. If the leaves are boiled in water and then cooled, the juice when placed on the skin takes away the sting. Dock leaves that usually grow nearby can also be rubbed into the skin to take away the burning sensation. It is said that the Roman soldiers brought nettle seeds with them to England in order to keep themselves warm in the cold damp winters. The story goes they would thrash their limb with the nettles to warm themselves up. Its Latin name urtica comes from the Latin uro which means to burn. Nettle itself comes from the Anglo-Saxon word of noed which means a sewing needle. There are over 500 species of nettle spread all over the world. Despite its sting, the nettle is full of vitamins and minerals and since ancient times has been used to enrich and flavour stews and soups.

Nettle comes into flower when summer has begun. It is as though this plant knows that the days will now become summery, warm and full of the strength of the sun. Nettle is full of this vibrant energy and shares this strength with the rest of the garden. If you place your hand near one of her leaves, you can feel a vibrancy. It seems as though the energy of the sun is being sent out to everything that surrounds her. It is as if the nettle, like the heart, has found a way to warm the spirits of everything around it. Even its sting tingles the skin with energy long after the pain has gone. It is no wonder that other plants closely group around her in order to receive this warmth and vitality.

Nettle loves company and sends a number of plants off each length of root, almost the more the merrier. They sway together in the wind and their seeds dance like some fine tiny bells laughing to the movement. Often nettles are surrounded by other plants and she twists and winds through whatever plants are around her. The plants look more vibrant and are fuller when there is a nettle among them. There is something generous, warm and vibrant about her company. Although she can sting, her leaves are very soft and tender to the touch.

It is said that the Great Lightening Serpent gave the nettle her sting. The Gypsies believe that nettles grow in places where there are underground passageways to where the fairies live. The nettle is believed to be a sacred plant to the thunder god Thor, and was thrown into the fire during storms as an offering to invoke protection and ward off danger. Nettles carried in the hand could keep ghosts away. If they were sprinkled on the ground around the house they were thought to keep evil spirits out. In folk medicine it was believed that if a bunch of freshly cut nettles were put under a sick person's bed it would help them to have a quick recovery. It was said a fever could be dispelled by pulling up a nettle by the roots and reciting the name of the ill person and their parents. Nettle was thought to make the heart merry, drive away melancholy and quicken the spirit.

Nettles like flax have a strong fibre from which paper and cloth can be made. It was used in the first world war to make soldiers' uniforms when cotton was in short supply. Nettle fibre was used in Scotland until very recently for napkins and tablecloths. It is used as twine for fishing nets and as a fine green dye for cloth.

Nettles are very rich in vitamins and minerals. Its tea is drunk by nursing mothers to stimulate the flow of milk and can be used to regulate menstruation. It is also drunk to help with gout and rheumatism. Culpepper recommended it as a blood tonic and purifier as well as for relieving high blood pressure and cystitis and as a gargle for mouth swelling. He also suggested that the seeds taken in alcohol could act as an antidote for poisonings. The infusion can be used externally for eczema and to promote hair growth. To stop bleeding or for septic wounds the dried leaves are used. Soaking nettle juice in cotton and then applying it to the skin is said to improve the circulation and the complexion. There are many stories about the success of nettles as a cure for rheumatism by a person stripping off naked and rolling in a bed of nettles in the spring.

In today's herbalism nettle is used to increase urination and the elimination of waste products. It helps many skin conditions such as childhood eczema. It is used for arthritis especially when fluid retention and poor kidney function are associated causes. Nettle slows or stops the bleeding of wounds and can be used to treat nosebleeds and heavy menstrual bleeding. Its ointment or juice is used to treat asthma, itchy skin, diaper rash and insect bites. Teas help anemia and improve breast milk production.

Nettles have traditionally been used in soups and vegetable puddings.

Nettle beer was made and drunk for pleasure and used as a cure for gout and rheumatism. Animals who are ill often eat nettles to help them recover. Added to feed the nettles help keep animals well nourished.

The heart circulates the nourishment, energy and vital forces throughout the body. In a similar sort of way nettle circulates energy throughout the gardens. Her tea warms our body and enlivens our spirits with her fiery energetic spirit. It is nettle's ability to transform sunshine and water and minerals into both warmth and vibrancy that gives her a special place in the garden. In this way she expresses the essence of summer itself. Summer creates the long days that give us warmth and energy so we have time to sit in the garden and have conversations with an ease that is not there at other times. We become tanned and healthy with the warmth and sunshine. It is as though a holiday has come to the world where we can give warmth and enjoyment to others. We are relaxed and at ease with all around us. This is how the nettle is with all the plants and flowers that grow around her in the garden.

When a flower bud has ripened with the abundance of warm summer sunshine then its case suddenly falls away and with silent mysterious movement a new brightly coloured flower unfolds itself. The caress of the sun is what opens the heart of each plant and that heart is expressed as an exquisite flower. Imagine this warmth, joy and love flowing into your heart so it too flowers with generosity and warmth in every encounter that comes. Nettle fills all around it with this warmth and generous energy full of love, kindness, and joy. Without this warmth there is often jealousy, coldness, and over-control. But when the sunshine returns and we feel our hearts loved and warmed, then the world becomes a summer evening full of the joy of good friends, food, laughter and enjoyment. This joy and warmth is the spirit of nettle whose vibrant energy brings alive our very heart strings as we too become an exquisite flower of love.

*'They talk in flowers and tell in a garland*
*their loves and cares.'*

James Percival

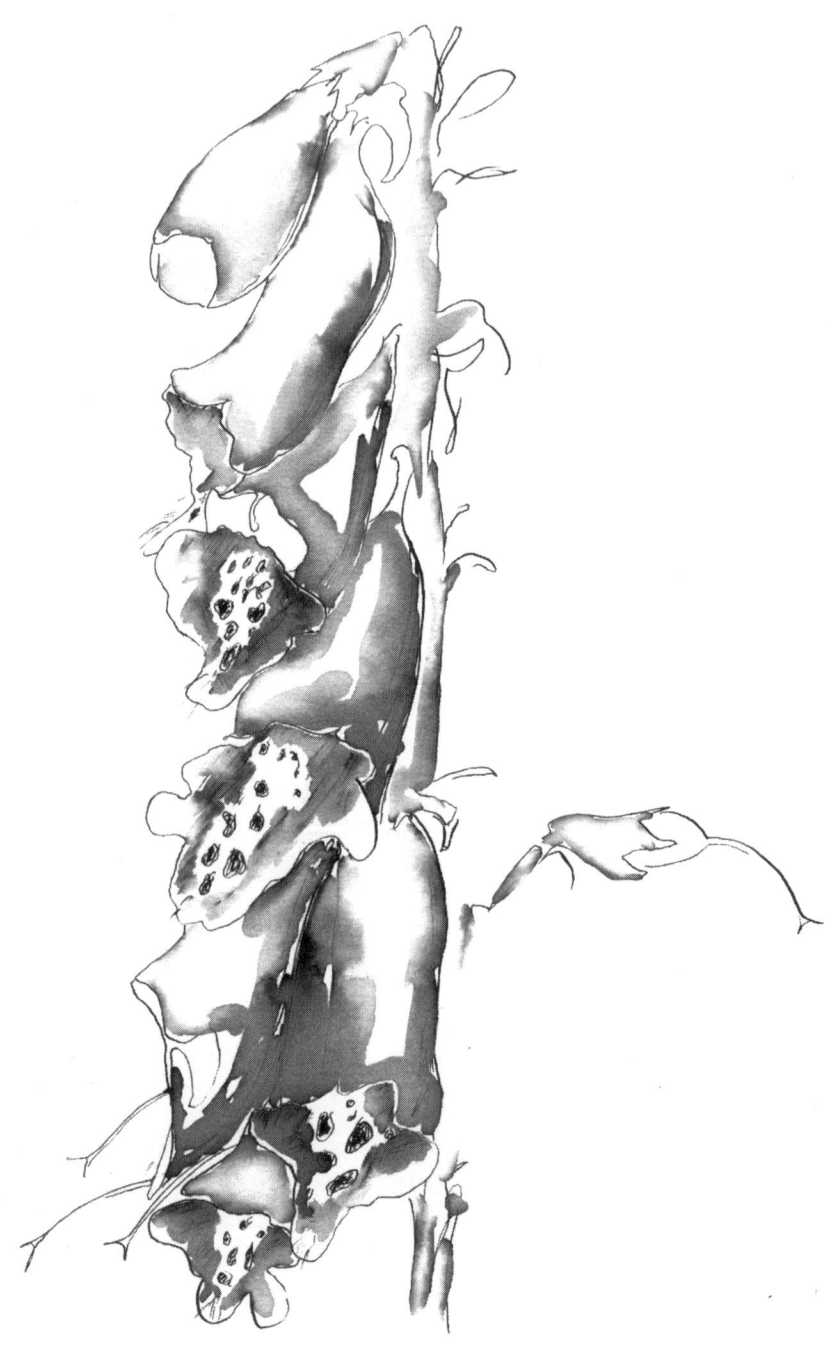

# FOXGLOVE
## *Digitalis Purpurea*

Foxglove is an enchanted flower. Her delicate soft green leaves form large fingers around her base. These balance the large single stem that holds the purple bell shaped flowers clustered together and flowing up the single stalk. They rise into the sky with the beauty of a bell steeple. These bells with their inner quilt-like patterns tempt all insects with a magnificent store of nectar and pollen. The flowers seem to smile, ring out and fly among the heavens with the beauty and delicateness of glove fingers. Foxglove is like a magnificent Italian bell tower strongly rooted in the earth and silhouetted against the sky. Her roots are fine but very strong and can balance her enormous height in very little soil. She is often seen growing on ledges or on steep slopes with the surefootedness of a mountain goat. Her purple flowers, delicate and soft to the touch have a lovely patterned tapestry woven inside enticing the insects to her rich chambers of nectar. As they taste the nectar they are showered with pollen to fertilize the seeds. Each bell will create hundreds of seeds from this pollination. For centuries she has been planted to give protection to the gardens and home. She has strength, balance and charm as well as a soft, vulnerable and velvety quality.

The Latin name, digitalis, comes from digitabulum which means a thimble or finger length and refers to the finger length bell flowers. The Anglo-Saxon name, fox gleow means fox glove. Gleow was an arched instrument hung with bells and perhaps describes the shape of the plant. The flowers are also called fairy flowers or fairy petticoats. The fairies were thought to hide in them and if the foxglove hung over, it was because the fairies were hiding in the bells. One of the stories for the name of foxglove says that the fairies were thought to give the bells to foxes to put on their feet so they could stalk poultry silently and escape the snares of man. The name could also have come about because the foxglove grows on woody slopes where fox burrows are found, and the foxes took the gloves themselves to surprise the chickens. The fox is thought to be a guide to the underworld with his intelligence and cunning.

In ancient times it was said that if foxglove was planted in the garden then the house and garden would be in harmony with all around and be protected. The plant was said to give mysterious powers to anyone who held it. It was also said that if you heard the bells of the foxglove ring then there would be an early death. The plant itself could be used to help a person contact the fairies, but their intentions would have to be pure. It was believed that carrying the flowers on a ship would bring bad luck.

Culpepper recommended using the leaves to heal fresh wounds and old sores. He also suggested a decoction to purge the body and open the liver and spleen. He was unaware of its use for heart failure. In the seventeenth century, a Dr Withering became curious about foxglove when a local herbalist gave it to help a person with heart failure where other medication had failed. The person was greatly helped. He did careful studies on doses and in the year he died it was established that digitalin reduces the pulse rate. There is a memorial to him in Edgbaston Old Church, Birmingham which has an engraved foxglove. Foxglove has been used for treating heart failure for over 200 years and is one of the native plants to be included in the British Pharmacoepia. Today a synthetic drug is used but recent studies suggest the synthetic form is more toxic. The use of foxglove has a tonic effect when the heart's ability to maintain normal circulation decreases. It enables the heart to beat more strongly, slowly and regularly. It also stimulates urination which lowers the strain on the heart.

Foxglove flowers at midsummer, and is nourished by the full heat and the warm loving heart of the sun. She enables this heart warmth of the garden to be protected and balanced so it can use the warmth, love, and energy of the fullness of the sunshine. She give strength and vitality back to the garden with great generosity, just as she gives an abundance of nectar to the bees. Foxglove has a great ability to stay balanced itself despite its height and in a similar way it is capable of balancing the heart warmth and spirit of the garden.

Somewhere deep in the forest is a place where willow trees grow alongside a gentle stream. The sunlight gently flutters on the woodland floor to the rhythms of the gentle winds. Here is a place that floxglove loves, where it is moist and fertile with just the right amount of sunshine. Imagine lying on the soft leaves at the base of the stem where your entire body feels comfortable and warm. Every part of your body is given the exact amount of softness and warmth that it needs. After a while your entire body feels in great harmony. From this place of balance you can feel at one with all that is around you.

Imagine this warmth and balance flowing into all your relationships. Now contact your heart. How does it feel to be held in this warmth and harmony. If the heart is too soft then the gates can close with more energy. If it is too hard then the gateways can be oiled to open more easily. If the heart is mistrustful then it can feel more confident. If it is small it can reach out more. If it is shy it can have a helping hand. If it is sad it can have some laughter.

Close your eyes and imagine digitalis standing in front of you. Ask it to harmonize the strings of your heart and give you something of love and joy for the coming year. Feel this difference deep inside and imagine how your relationships might ease. Feel the temperature of your heart and its openness. Spend some time in the bell tower of digitalis and feel her softness and joy. Imagine this in your life. Imagine being so comfortable and balanced that it is easy to relate on all levels. When you are ready come back open your eyes. Thank digitalis for her gifts and offer her a gift in return. Digitalis uses the warmth and light of the sun to bring balance, harmony and protection to the heart. It is like putting on the gloves of her flowers that protect us from harm and extremes of temperature. It is this protection and balancing that lies at the centre of the spirit of digitalis.

*'A flower unplucked is but left to the falling
and nothing is gained by not gathering roses.'*

Robert Frost

*'A brotherhood is as a cluster of grapes,
when you squeeze them they become one juice.'*

Mevlana Jelaluddin Rumi

# EVENING PRIMROSE
## *Oenothera Biennis*

Evening primrose blossoms in the height of the summer sun. Her luscious green leaves and tall stalks produce multiple green buds that suddenly open into large buttery flowers. The flowers close during the day when it is too warm and open in the evening temping a great variety of insects. Their colour is like liquid sun food full of satisfaction. The flowers themselves smell of sweet musk and are full of the bee foods of nectar and pollen. Everything about evening primrose is plentiful and nourishing including her large wholesome roots. When the seed heads form they too are full of nourishing oils. It is as though she is expressing the abundance of mother earth herself with her rich milky roots, her broad green leaves full of water and sunshine, her blossoms full of nectar and her seeds full of nutrients and oils. No matter how high she grows, she remains well rooted and stable, secure in her relationship with mother earth.

Its Latin name oenothera biennis comes from two Greek words, oinos meaning wine and thera meaning a hunt. It seems to be an old name that Theophrastus gave to certain plants because the large roots were made into a relish that was eaten with wine to dispel the effects of the wine in the same way olives are eaten. The roots are still eaten today and the French use both the root and flowers for garnishing salads. The flowers are also used to decorate cakes and garnish cold dishes. The leaves, because of their rich mineral content were named the ham of the gardener and the plant given the gardening name of 'jambon du jardinier'. The leaves, flowers and roots can also be used to flavour vinegar. The roots are still made into a salty, vinegary relish that is eaten as an aperitif with wine. Evening primrose is one of the grand culinary wild plants of the garden.

The American Indians used evening primrose in various ways. They would rub it on their moccasins and bodies to guarantee a good hunt. This technique was also good for keeping snakes away. They bruised and soaked the plant leaves for wound dressings and to relieve bruises and other skin problems. They used the fine black seeds as food and a healing medicine. Roots were steamed as vegetables or roasted. They were also made into teas used to treat obesity, aid digestion, calm skin disorders and help clear skin.

The plant is used in modern herbalism in various ways. The bark and leaves gathered in the second year after the flowers have blossomed have been used in the treatment of whooping cough. Because they are a mild sedative they have also been taken for digestive problems and asthma. The oil can be used externally for eczema and other itchy skin conditions. In recent times the oil taken internally has resulted in lowering blood pressure and also preventing the clumping of platelets. The oil is now also taken for premenstrual problems as well as abdominal bloating. The oil taken internally may also benefit multiple sclerosis, rheumatoid arthritis and other problems related to the circulation.

In your mind's eye see the time just before sunset when the sun is a rich golden colour and the activity of the garden has calmed. There are rich ripe purple grapes on the vines and in the valley below the ripened wheat is golden in colour. The pumpkins are a reddish orange and the apples a rosy red and yellow. The red squirrels are leaping along the branches of the walnut tree gathering nuts for the winter. In this golden light, the flowers of evening primrose open giving the insects a final sweet treat for the end of the day.

Imagine you are in a golden field of wheat at harvest time with a rich golden sun ripening all the fruits on the trees. In the middle of the field there is a woven basket filled with harvest fruits and vegetables. Suddenly you find yourself sitting on the lap of mother earth herself able to have all of the great harvest you see all around you. Ask the spirit of evening primrose for a harvest fruit. Taste the fruit and feel its nourishment flow through your entire system. Ask yourself what you have harvested over the past year and what you need to nourish yourself with over the next months. Feel safe and secure knowing that there will be food and nourishment for the next year. Thank evening primrose for her basket of goodness

Here is the great stored bounty of the kingdom so all can have the comfort and reserves to get through the winter. Here you can receive great fullness and feel the great oneness of the earth who nourishes all without thought and with great all enveloping care. Here is the security and stability of mother earth who gives us a place for both our homes and to grow our food. Here is the earth's granary, her great storehouse, and her comfortable residence. This abundant splendour is the spirit of evening primrose.

'*Earth laughs in flowers*'

Ralph Waldo Emerson

'*The earth does not belong to us;*
*we belong to the earth,*
*and we have a sacred duty to protect her*
*and return thanks for the gifts of life.*'

Oren Lyons

# Great Mullein
## *Verbascum Thapsus*

As the first leaves of great mullein appear they form a rosette of soft grey-green. As the leaves grow larger a central stalk grows upwards that then branches out in all directions. The delicate yellow flowers emerge in abundance all along these out-reaching arms. The mullein in this way becomes another great giant of the garden but one that is full of great softness and vitality expressed by its flowers and leaves that blossom in every direction. The flowers seem to take in the vibrant sunshine of midsummer and send the energy outwards as more and more petals and leaves appear. The leaf system is arranged in such a way that the smaller leaves at the top, drop dew or rain water into the leaves below so that all moisture is directed towards the roots.

Its central stem is strong and fibrous and in ancient times was used as a lamp wick. The stalks were dipped into suet to make candles for funerals and ceremonies. For this reason it is sometimes called 'Our Lady's Candle'. Its Latin name verbascum comes from the root of barba meaning beard probably named because of the hairiness of its leaves. Both in Anglo-Saxon and old French, moleyn or mullein comes from malandrian. Malandre was a lung disease and the leaves in ancient times were used as a remedy for lung diseases in both cows and people. Mullein tea was used for coughs and colds but needed to be strained so the hairs would not irritate the mouth. The Anglo-French moleine also goes back to the Latin word mollis which means soft.

In Greek mythology Ulysses arrived at the Island of Dawn ruled by the goddess Circe who was skilled in all forms of enchantment. Some of his men went to her palace and as they ate they were transformed into swine. When the only man to survive came back to tell him what had happened, Ulysses seized his sword to go and rescue his men. On his way he met the god Hermes who gave him great mullein as a charm against Circe's enchantments. Although Circe tried to enchant him, the flowers protected him. She finally promised to release all of his men and in turn he gave her three sons. Circe also told him how to find the seer Teiresias in Hades to find out how his fortunes would go. Since this time Mullein has been used to drive away evil spirits and enchantments. It is also used by 'wise women' for protection at sacred festivals such as the solstices and equinoxes. In medieval times it was used as one of the herbs of protection that was hung over doorways. Today it is still said that a garden with mullein growing in it is blessed. It is also said that it brings its good naturedness to the garden. Mullein is associated with the feast day of St Fiaere on August 30th, who is the patron saint of gardens.

In Roman times the leaves were placed in sandals that were worn down to cushion the feet. Figs were wrapped in the leaves to keep them from rotting. The long stems were used by soldiers as torches and were later dipped in wax or tallow and used as candles in ceremonies. The leaves were smoked both for the cough of consumption as well as in sacred ceremonies for ancestral knowledge. The seeds were said to intoxicate fish and were used by fishermen. An infusion of the flowers was used by Roman woman to dye their hair a golden colour. Soap made from mullein ash was said to restore grey hair to its normal colour. Since ancient times mullein has been used for lung problems. The leaves or flowers can be made into a tea or infusion and help coughs, colds, and bronchitis. Gerard recommended it as a cough medicine.

Mullein is used in various ways today. Its flowers can be placed in olive oil for 21 days and then the oil is strained and used for ear infections and skin infections. It is also used for frostbite and bruises. Externally the leaves can be applied as a good wound healer. Mullein oil is a valuable destroyer of disease germs. The oily substance in the leaves can be used as a poultice for chest infections. A decoction of mullein, sage, marjoram and chamomile put in the bath is said to be good for colds, stiff joints and cramps. Distilled water of the flowers is said to be good for burns. An infusion made with the leaves and flowers has slightly sedative properties. If the leaves are placed in shoes it is said that mullein keeps the feet warm and prevents the person from getting a cold. Carrying a piece of mullein provides protection and is said to attract favours of the opposite sex. If leaves or flowers are placed in a pillow then there will be no nightmares.

In ancient China there was a system of messengers who would run certain distances and then hand on the message or parcel to the next runner. In this way the Emperor could be in contact with all of his kingdom as was necessary. One day the Emperor had a very special package to be carried to the other side of the Empire. At first he gave it to one of his horsemen. This horseman rode for the first day guarding the package with his cloak.

He covered a great distance by three times changing horses. He handed the package to a monk who walked through the mountains at night trusting in the heavenly father. In the morning it was given to the boat man on the river who took it down stream through the great flowing waters of vitality. That night it was placed on a ship sailing by the stars. At last it reached the Emperor's daughter who opened the parcel containing an ancient healing text. She was able to use the plants to heal her child of a great fever.

Imagine being on a canal boat. Here you are able to travel through the countryside carrying goods from place to place as they are needed. Now imagine these passageways within. Our inner body is constantly transporting food, blood and other materials throughout the body. In such a way all of the body can receive what nourishment it needs as and when it needs it. The heart needs blood, warmth and love, the stomach needs food, liquids and care, and the small intestine needs the nutrients from the stomach to sort into what is for use and what is for elimination. This circulation of nourishment and goods is the spirit of great mullein who is the great circulator of energy throughout the garden.

*'The space between heaven and earth is like a bellows,*
*The shape changes but the form is the same*
*The more it moves, the more it yields.'*

Lao Tsu

# PLANTAIN
## *Plantago*

Plantain is a very humble plant that grows close to the ground. It has very rich green leaves that reach upwards towards the heavens. Its roots are multiple fingers that skillfully hold the soil in place. The leaves gather in the richness from the sun, rain and air and place it into the soil through these very fine roots. Its leaves being either broad or narrow are firmly rooted in the ground and from this strength reach upwards towards the heavens as though celebrating the rich wonders of the sky above. Each plant then produces stems that grow tall and straight until they swell at the tip and open into tiny flowers with twinkling suspended stamens just waiting to be pollinated. These suspended morsels seem to shine like tiny stars. The whole stem is like a magic fairy wand that dances in the wind and sunlight. It is amazing how such a tiny plant can inspire the imagination. Indeed it is simple plantain that has the spirit to both let go and inspire

The plant itself, although appearing small and delicate can be stepped on, crushed, cut and bent but will still come back after a rain shower and regrow its seed stalk again and again. It is like a head, straight, special, elegant and suitably crowned with stars with its leaves reaching up in wonder at the heavens above. In Scotland the plant has the name of slanlus which means the plant of healing because of a belief in its healing virtues. In Ireland it was used to treat wounds and bruises. The native Americans called it the Englishman's foot because it seemed to spring up from the footsteps of white settlers. It was one of the plants that was carried with settlers for healing. It is used on the solstice as one of the plants for protection. In ancient times the stems were said to tell of future lovers.

Pliny went so far as to say that if plantain 'be put into a pot where many pieces of flesh are boiling, it will sodden them together'. He also said it will cure the madness of dogs. It has the name of snakeweed because of its supposed healing qualities in the cases of bites from venomous creatures. Indeed a Dr Robinson once reported that an Indian in America received a great reward from the Assembly of South Carolina for his discovery that the plantain was the chief remedy for the 'cure of the rattlesnake'. For the Saxons it was one of the nine sacred plants. It was also eaten as a salad herb.

A decoction was said to be good for the lungs and throat. It was said to be good for obstructions of the liver, spleen and kidneys. It was used to cool inflammations of the eyes and to ease pains in the ear. The leaves were used for cuts and bruises. Oil from the seeds was said to ease headaches and to be good for lunatics. Culpepper says that plantain water is good for spreading scabs, ringworm, and shingles among other things. As a folk remedy it was said plantain should be bound with red wool to the head to cure headaches and could be placed beneath the feet to ease weariness. Placing a bit of the root in a pocket was said to protect from snake bite.

In modern herbology plantain is used in many ways. Plantain leaves are used to quickly staunch the blood flow and encourage the repair of damaged tissues. It is also used, like comfrey in treating bruises, burns and broken bones. Made into an ointment it can be used for haemorrhoids, fistulae, and ulcers. When it is taken internally it helps with gastritis, peptic ulcers, diarrhoea, dysentery, irritable bowel syndrome, respiratory congestion, loss of voice and uninary tract bleeding.

Once there was a single plant of plantain in an entire field of grass. As it grew upward it watched the sun cross the sky and the stars turning in the night sky. Everywhere it saw changes. It watched the seasons come and go, each transforming into the next. The plant knew that each year it would produce beautiful flowers and seeds. These would then be let go of to be scattered by the winds and create new plants. Letting go was a part of each moment. One night a bright star shown just above the little plant. An angel came down. Together they talked about the changes on earth. The little plant of plantain realized that by letting go of his seeds, which was his special talent, there would be more and more plants that would delight in the heavens and that the heavens could shine upon and inspire. With the angel he watched the night pass and at dawn the angel flew back to the heavens. In his heart the little plant knew now that the angel was always there and he was no longer alone..

The great sky above us is often thought to represent the heavenly father. Imagine this great father listening carefully to what you have to say. You tell him what has happened in each day and share with him your hopes and dreams. Imagine being taken up into his heavenly kingdom and being able to see further than you have ever been able to see before. You are able to see other countries, other people, other ideas and other sides of the questions you have asked. Imagine walking through the heavenly gardens and the palace itself with its rooms of wealth and comfort.

Now imagine you are contained somewhere without any contact. You feel alone and empty. Slowly a door opens and the kindest most gentle hand full of warmth and love comes and is offered to you. You walk out into the sunshine and talk together. You tell the gentle man your story and then with his encouragement you change the parts of the story that are holding you back or are no longer useful. You feel yourself lighter and more confident. Then you tell this kind man about who you really are. Maybe you begin by saying who you are not and then find the things that you are and can do.

It is the spirit of plantain that brings back our connection to the special person we are by letting go of what is no longer useful. Here we refind our connection to the heavens above and place our hand in the great father's hand knowing that he has carefully listened to all we have to say. Here that deep aloneness that lives inside us all has been listened to and we in turn have been inspired in what is possible in our lives. With plantain we find our own heavenly essence with its warm currents and purpose. We can rest in the heavenly palace and its welcome fragrances that are now a part of our own inner resource.

*'The garden is the home of the nightingale.*
*The dung heap is suitable to the beetle.*

Mevlana Jelaluddin Rumi

# HEATHER
## *Erica*

Heather creates a fantastic carpet of fresh innocent white flowers in the spring and rich soft purple flowers in the autumn. The white flowers are often gathered by travellers as a lucky charm and for protection. Because of its place in the mountains, the purple heather is often thought of as representing beauty through its flowers, solitude because of the time it blossoms and inspiration because of its colours. This woody plant is full of tiny bell like flowers. Its leaves are sturdy but soft to the touch. Its fragrance is delicate like dark sugar. It is a robust plant that flowers at the seasonal changes to the great delight of the bee. It gathers the fullness of the sun and concentrates it into pure sweetness for the bees at a time when other flowers are scarce. It gives a fragrant sweet taste to the honey and helps the bees' reserves in early spring and autumn. In the same way it helps our spirit reserves before the long winter. Seeing a hillside full of heather in the fall is like falling into a sea of purple waves enriching and warming our hearts before the cold wintry weather.

Its seeds can remain dormant for over ten years waiting for the right conditions. After a forest fire it is one of the first plants to return, producing thousands of seedlings. In ancient times the root stock was made into musical pipes. Until recent times the plant itself was gathered to make mattress stuffing. Heather flowers are still placed under pillows or in herb pillows to give deep sleep. Its name calluna comes from the Greek kalluna which means to brush. It was often used as a broom and hence its name.

Heather is one of the flowers that is sacred to the goddess Venus and the Egyptian Goddess Isis. Isis's brother Osiris was placed in heather at Byblos where she went to find him. In Ireland as legend goes, the giantess Garbh Ogh at the time of her death set her chair amidst the blossoming heather in the womb of the hills. At sunset she faded into the hillside protecting the country around her ever after. It is said that when burned, heather can conjure up ghosts and make it rain. The flowers since ancient times have been used to brew ale. Heather ale was said to have restorative properties. Apparently when the Norse invaded the Picts in the fourth century, despite torture not one Pict would reveal the secret of heather ale. Heather flowers are also said to preserve youth. Because of this, dew was gathered at the full moon or water was infused with the flowers and used on the skin. It is said to benefit the complexion and rid it of freckles. Heather blossoms were used to make a tea that was a good overall tonic. Adding the tips of flowering shoots to herbal drinks and beer was said to purify the blood.

Today heather is used in many ways. The tips of heather gathered in the autumn are used for making poultices for easing the aches and pains of rheumatism. The macerated flowering tips produce a lineament that can be rubbed on affected joints. In modern herbalism heather is used as a cleansing and detoxifying herb that can be taken as an urinary antiseptic and diuretic, disinfecting the urinary tract and mildly increasing urine production. It is also used to treat cystitis and inflammatory bladder infections as well as for kidney and bladder stones. A hot poultice of heather tips is a folk remedy for chilblains.

According to Bach, heather people are always concerned about themselves which has the effect of exhausting the listener. It comes from a deep need to talk about themselves and their problems. However once the inner vitality has been restored then someone who has suffered is able to listen to and help others. As Bach says, such a person then is able to put his difficulties behind him and become absorbed in the problems of others and is unsparing in his efforts to help them.

Heather is just such a plant to help a person let go of the old in order to be able to take in the new. Heather appears in spring to inspire the world after the harshness of winter and comes again in the autumn to give a final burst of beauty to all around as the seasons again change. Nature knows how to let go with each season. Autumn drops its leaves into the ground and winter breaks them up so all the nutrients can seep into the ground. Spring comes and awakens the seeds with warmth. Summer ripens the fruits and the harvest season produces the new seeds that will bring new life in the next spring. We too have a need to let go of the unused leaves of our lives and to transform those experiences into new material to nourish new beginnings that grow into greater experience that matures our knowledge and understanding of life. It is the spirit of heather that helps to bring about these transformations by helping us to let go of what is not needed. We then can flower in the changing season inspired by the space that has been left open and somehow freed.

There is a story told of a man who finds a horse and all his neighbours say how lucky he is. But the next day his son falls from the horse and breaks his leg. So the neighbours say how unfortunate that is. But a week later all the young men of the town have to go to fight for the Sultan except the young man who has broken his leg. Then the horse eats the carrots in a neighbours field which the man has to pay for. But then the neighbour dies and the man grazes his horse on the land. The son then turns the land into gardens and the horse helps to plow the fields. It is not what happens in life but our ability to deal with the changes that is important. Heather allows us to blossom through those changes.

*'Who can wait quietly while the mud settles?*
*Who can remain still until the moment of action?*
*Observers of the Tao are not swayed by desire for change.'*

Lao Tsu

# HORSETAIL
## *Equisetum Arvense*

Horsetail loves water. Where it grows is supposed to indicate subterranean, flowing waters or springs. It grows delicately out of the ground in segmented sections from which grow great green hairs. Its segmented stem has skirts of these flexible green hairs that create an image of a great green fountain. The stems themselves can be taken apart and then put back together again. It is a primitive plant like the bamboo and is a descendent of the huge trees that lived in the paleozoic era between 600 and 375 million years ago. These were fern like trees of several meters high segmented in the same way horsetail is today. Its beautiful green joined stems that grow these long bristly hairs has earned it the name of bottle-bush, paddock-pipes and mare's tail. The plant has both fertile and sterile stems. The fertile stem appears in spring and grows straight up without branches. It has a cone like catkin which produces spores that are released as the stem dries. It can also reproduce from its roots. The sterile stem is hollow except at the joints where  there are long bristly hairs. These stems are full of silicone which were used to scour pans and polish metal. They were also tied to the tails of cows to help them swat flies. In addition they were used for scouring pewter ware and wooden kitchen utensils, as well as cow milk pails and to put the final touches on combs and arrows. It is called the woodcarver's sandpaper.

In Roman times the young fertile shoots were fried with flour and butter. Whistles made of the stems were thought to be able to call snakes. When placed in the bedroom it was thought to increase fertility. From ancient times horsetail has been considered a wound healing herb. Gerard says the dried plant when placed on a wound will heal it even if the sinews have been cut.

It is used in many ways today. It is an excellent clotting agent. It can be used to staunch wounds, to stop nosebleeds and can reduce the coughing up of blood. It also has an effect on the urinary system and is used for cystitis, urethritis, and prostate disease. Horsetail speeds up the repair of damage to connective tissue and improves both its strength and elasticity. The herb can be added to a bath to benefit slow healing sprains and fractures as well as help with eczema and acne. It can be used as a gargle for oral infections. It has been used to treat rheumatic and arthritic problems, emphysema and for chronic swelling of the legs

This ancient plant has the ability to fill our reserves and reservoirs with the energy and fluidity of water. At times when there has been no rain there is great fear that all will die. It is a feeling of relief when the rains come again and the cracked earth regains its greenness. Imagine a drop of water diving from a great water fall without any harmful changes or this same drop flowing through a great river to the sea. Water can flow swiftly and can also be very calm. It is both forceful and unstoppable, as well as gentle and still. It can be divided and then return to itself flowing fully once again. Without water nothing can grow or live. Water nourishes, energizes and replenishes every cell in the body. It also cleanses and washes out all impurities. When the summer has been dry there is a lusciousness that comes with the rains. All is fresh and green and the flowers return for a second flowering.

It was out of the primordial seas that all life originally came. Water holds this primitive energy of life. Water also holds the imprint of where it has been. In this way deep source waters are vibrantly full of the riches that lie underground. The spirit of horsetail refreshes us like a bubbling spring, a great mountain stream, a returning current and a valley full of river waters.

Imagine being water in the form of drops of rain refreshing the earth. Allow those droplets to become a river gradually growing larger and stronger passing through entire countries until coming to the sea. Then become the great sea containing the forceful tidal movements and fishes. Become the storms and waves of water full of energy. Then be a calm clear lake reflecting the moonlight or a deep well of water in the middle of the desert. Then imagine being a spring bursting out of the ground into an ancient stone basin. Feel the fluidity, vitality, and constant flow that is water. This is what the spirit of horsetail brings into our lives.

*'There is no quiet place in the white man's cities.*
*What is there to life if a man cannot hear the lonely cry of the*
*whippoowill or the arguments of the frogs around the pool at night?'*

Chief Seattle

*'Under heaven nothing is softer and more yielding than water.*
*And for attacking the solid and strong, nothing is better,*
*It has no equal.'*

Lao Tsu

# MALLOW
## *Malva Sylvestris*

Mallow dances in all directions around the garden. Her bright purple flowers are delicately striped and look like fine bone china cups. The leaves are a fine green velvet and the root is strong and tuberous. She has great strength in her roots and from this strength the rest of the plant is able to move in all directions and around and through whatever surrounds it. It is this flexibility that sculpts the plant's amazing variations in forms. Both the garden hollyhock and hibiscus are members of this same family The fruits that follow in the autumn have been given the name cheeses because their shape resembles a round cheese. In ancient times these were eaten or sprinkled onto salads. They have a nutty taste. This plant excels in softness both to the eye and the touch. It grows in full sunlight and can survive with little water, but with rain and shade it grows with abandoned lushness.

Its Greek name malvaceae comes from malake which means soft and refers to its ability to soften and heal. The generic name althaea comes from the Greek word altho which means to cure. The plant is said to represent humanity and beneficence. There is an old Spanish belief that says that a kitchen garden and mallow are sufficient medicine for the home. Mallow was one of the flower pollens that was scattered over a Neanderthal man buried in a cave in Iraq over 6,000 years ago. It was believed to strengthen the man on his journey to the next world. Carrying a piece of mallow was said to make a departed lover remember you or to attract a new love. The Druids believed that the seeds gathered during a full moon could be made into an ointment for virility.

From ancient times the plant has been eaten as it is totally devoid of any unwholesome properties. The young flowers and leaves were eaten as a delicacy by the Romans. They used the leaves in barley soup and for stuffing of pigs and to make a fragrant vinegar. The Greeks and Armenians in times of drought would live off herbs one of which was the mallow. The leaves and flowers were eaten either cooked or raw. The root was boiled and then fried with onions and butter. Pliny said of the mallow 'Whoever shall take a spoonful of the mallow shall that day be free from all disease that may come to him'. In France the young leaves and flowers are still eaten in spring salads to stimulate the kidneys. A syrup is also made for the same purpose. Early Arab physicians would use the leaves as a poultice for inflammation. It was used to reduce swelling and to draw out toxins. The roots were given to babies to chew to help with teething. In France sweets are made from the root that help to soothe a sore chest, coughs and hoarseness. It is sometimes mixed with eucalyptus for coughs and other chest ailments. The flowers are used as a tea for colds as well as to decorate cakes and salads.

The roots when boiled in water give a mucous like matter. This helps when the natural mucus has been lost, such as in the intestines, stomach and lungs. Mallow is in this way useful in inflammation and irritation of the alimentary canal, and in the urinary and respiratory organs. It is also effective for bruises, sprains or any ache in the muscles or sinews. Boiled in milk it is a popular remedy for coughs, bronchitis, whooping cough and colds. The powdered or crushed fresh roots make a good poultice for inflammation. The fresh leaves steeped in hot water can be used to reduce inflammation, bruises and bee or wasp stings.

In modern herbalism the flowers boiled in water with a little honey is a good gargle for sore throats. Mallow soothes and protects the mucous membranes. This means that the root counters excess stomach acid, peptic ulceration and gastritis. It is also mildly laxative and beneficial for many intestinal problems including ileitis, colitis, diverticulitis and irritable bowel syndrome. It can also be used to treat cystitis and frequent urination. The flowers can be used either fresh or crushed in a warm infusion for inflamed skin. The root can also be used in an ointment for boils or abscesses. The peeled root maybe given as a chew stick to teething babies.

Mallow like horsetail has the fluidity and vitality of water. Here are the storehouses of reserves, the reservoirs of winter rains, the freshness of morning dew, the brightness of raindrops on leaves after a storm and the rainbows full of colour after spring showers. Imagine being parched from lack of water and then suddenly having your reserves filled with heavenly rains. Feel the refreshment of having your spirit filled with vibrant spring waters. Allow yourself to be bathed in the dewy freshness of the morning air. Mallow has these reservoirs and resources of fluidity and energy. This not only rejuvenates the body but also the spirit. When the spirit is resourced, refreshed and revitalized then our lives are filled with beauty and have a fullness and a pleasure. We are penetrated with vitality just like fine rains penetrate the earth to make it grow its wonders again. When our resources are full we too can dance around the garden like mallow.

*'No occupation is so delightful to me as the culture of the earth..*
*and no culture comparable to that of a garden..*
*But though an old man, I am but a young gardener.'*

Thomas Jefferson

*'The highest good is like water,*
*Water gives life to all things and does not strive,*
*It flows everywhere and so is like the Tao.'*

Lao Tsu

# YARROW
## *Achillea Millefolium*

Yarrow has fine delicate lace-like bunches of flowers surrounded by soft green feather-like leaves. In the late summer when the sides of roads have been cut back and cleared, the beautiful feathery leaves of yarrow grow again like tiny ferns. Suddenly out of the centre of this delicate green bed comes a bunch of white flowers arranged like old lace. It has a strong pungent scent like old cotton packed in musty lavender. It loves the strong sunshine of summer and continues to flower until autumn even if it is cut. The flowers and leaves give the appearance of great sensitivity that gives strength. In this same way, lace is delicate but so finely woven it can last centuries.

The plant's Greek name achillea comes from the name of Achilles. In Greek mythology Chiron the centaur knew the plant lore of all the woodlands. He was said to have the wisdom and heart of a man with the swift power of a horse. It was he who showed Achilles how to make a salve to heal his warriors' wounds at the battle of Troy. It is said that Achilles scraped some rust off his spear into the wound of Telephus and bound it with yarrow to help it heal. It was called the military herb by the ancients. Its name millefolium means a thousand leaves and refers to the many feathery leaves of the plant. Yarrow comes from the Anglo Saxon word gearwe and means to prepare or to be ready. In this way is does act as a defense against other ills.

The stems of the yarrow were used by the Druids to divine the seasonal weather. In China they are still cut and used as the fifty I Ching sticks to foretell the future. Through the centuries it has been used to help with divination and clairvoyance and was one of the plants used at Delphi to put the high priestess into a trance. It was a powerful herb in Anglo-saxon times and was used in divination rituals and as a charm against bad luck and illness. When worn, yarrow is said to protect the wearer and when held in the hand it is said to stop all fear and grant courage. Carrying yarrow is also said to bring love and to attract friends or relatives who you most want to see.

Yarrow has been traditionally used to heal wounds. The native American Indians used it to staunch wounds and help fight infections They called it wound medicine. An ointment was made in Scotland from early times to heal cuts and bruises. In the middle ages it was used to treat burns and wounds. Yarrow tea was said to dispel melancholy. When yarrow was placed over the bed of newly weds it was said to bring enduring love. If carried in a wedding bouquet it was said to ensure seven years of happiness. A bit of yarrow placed under a pillow at night was thought to bring a vision of a future husband or wife. Washing the head with yarrow infusion will help prevent baldness but will not cure it if it has already begun.

Yarrow lowers blood pressure, strengthens the walls of the blood vessels and is useful for slow healing wounds. A salve of yarrow helps ulcers and varicose veins while a decoction helps wounds, chapped skin, eczema, and rashes. It cleanses the whole body and helps with colds. It can calm inflamed gums and chewing on a leaf will help reduce toothache. Yarrow tea is a good remedy for colds and fevers. It is said to be good for baldness if the head is washed with it. Culpepper says that boiling it in white wine helps the kidneys, regulates menstruation and reduces blood pressure  He said if a leaf of yarrow was pulled off by the left hand as a sick person's name was said, the sickness would be taken away.

In modern times yarrow is used to arrest both internal and external bleeding. It helps to regulate the menstrual cycle, reduces heavy bleeding and eases menstrual pain. It also helps with colds and the flu. It is useful for weak digestion and colic. It can help hay fever, lower high blood pressure as well as improve venous circulation and tone varicose veins.

Yarrow has great strength and direction. Imagine the dawn piercing the horizon with pale rose light. Suddenly you are mounting a fine stallion feeling its mighty strength under your weight. You feel its warmth, animal strength and primitive smell. All this you can guide and harness to move in great directions. You begin to ride slowly until both you and the horse are flying across the landscape in full gallop. You reach new horizons with an ease you never had before. Suddenly you climb a hill and resting at the top you can see the fullness of all that surrounds you.

Feel the strength and power of this horse that you are riding across the plains. Feel the graceful energy and speed beneath you. Here is a freedom of energy to move in all directions. Here our feet have a swiftness and fleetness of a mighty horse. Yarrow allows our energy to flow with great strength and vitality so we have the sight, purpose and strength to achieve our goals. Here we are fully in the saddle guiding our energy towards its goal no matter what the weather brings. Here the gateways are open and we have the ability to divine the future and bring it to fruition. Here the great resource of the sea of chi feeds our hopes and dreams and moves them into action. We are fuelled by this energy of our horse that both guides and brings surprises to the unfolding of life.

*'The work of a garden bears visible fruits*
*in a world where most of our labours seem suspiciously meaningless.'*

Pam Brown

# MUGWORT
## *Artemisia Vulgaris*

Mugwort or artemisia grows all over the world in many different varieties including the common french tarragon, the large wild wormwood and the tiny alpine and desert plants. Her leaves are irregular because she comes from prehistoric times. They are bright green on top and a softer velvety colour underneath. When planted in the garden she harmonizes the energy around her. Her roots spread easily and like horsetail she needs to be contained. She spends all summer slowly growing and absorbing the warmth and sunshine of the summer sun. It is not until very late summer that her tiny but numerous flowers appear giving bees and insects a special treat before the long winter. Even in the cold of winter her tiny shoots remain green. She is a plant that has the ability to both absorb and extend the great energy she acquires from the sun. Because of this she is a plant that has been used for healing all over the world for centuries.

Her name artemisia comes from the goddess Artemis who was the goddess of the wilderness. She is the goddess who protects women in child birth as well as the one who protects the sacred space in ancient rituals. She is wild and untameable, being a virgin aloof from entanglements. She is the initiation into the naked beauty of the wild places. She is the goddess of the doorway between life and death, this world and the invisible world beyond. Mugwort is this raw energy and when used can undo the stagnant blocks and enhance the harmonic flow of energy again.

Mugwort was placed on or near a woman when giving birth to protect her and the baby. The common name of mugwort is said to come from moughte meaning moth. This comes from the time it was used to protect against moths. But it could also get its name from mug as it was used to flavour drinks such as beer and ales. Another possibility is from the old English word of mucgwyrt which means midge wort referring to its insect repelling properties. In ancient times it was believed to keep the traveller from fatigue, sunstroke, wild beasts and evil spirits. It was also carried to increase lust and fertility, to prevent backache, and to cure disease and madness. In China it is hung over the door to prevent bad spirits from entering the house. On the solstice the Celts would wear garlands and girdles of mugwort for protection while dancing around the bonfire. The garlands would be cast into the fire as protection for the coming year. Roots of mugwort placed over the door was thought to ward off diseases and bad luck. They also believed it was a herb of clairvoyance and was taken as a tea to aid divination. If it was placed by the bed or placed in a pillow it was said to aid prophetic dreams. The Roman soldiers placed leaves in their shoes so they would not become weary on their journeys and would be protected from lightening, wild beasts and poisons. It was even worn by St John the Baptist as a girdle of protection when he went into the wilderness. The dried leaves have been smoked as well as used as tea and for poultry stuffing.

Culpepper says mugwort makes an excellent tea for female disorders. He also says the fresh juice is a remedy for too much opium. Gerard says that mugwort can cure the shakings of the joints and was an old fashioned popular remedy for epilepsy and hysterical fits. Its oil kills worms, resists poison and is good for the liver and jaundice.

Mugwort is today mainly used as a digestive and tonic herb  A decoction when taken, can help to improve the appetite, digestive function and the absorption of nutrients. It can also encourage the elimination of worms, as well as increasing bile flow and mildly inducing the onset of menstruation. It is used as an antiseptic as well as in the treatment of malaria. Used with pellitory of the wall it can be made into a poultice to ease all outward pains. When it is placed among woollen clothes it prevents and destroys moths. Used in the bath artemisia will refresh and revive.

The Chinese and Japanese have for centuries used artemisia for healing. It is gathered on both the summer and winter solstice and dried for two years. It is then rolled into cigar like sticks and then lit and passed over the place of discomfort. This loose moxa, as it is called in acupuncture, can also be made into little cones which are placed directly on the acupuncture points to warm them before a needle is used. It is said to gently warm the spirit of the point so when it is contacted with the needle it can give the most benefit to the patient.

Mugwort is the vibrant green man of the garden. She knows every pattern of energy that flows through life. When planted in the garden all the plants around benefit from her ability to balance and harmonize. Lie in the centre of this great garden and feel the cold quiet stillness of winter, the vibrant uninhibited movement of spring, the warmth and ease of summer, the fullness of the harvest and the inspiration and letting go of the autumn. Feel joy, sorrow, sympathy, anger and fear. Move from one energy to the next with inspiration and harmony. It is mugwort that can bring harmony and balance to whatever energy is in excess or in deficiency. Here is nature's very ability to grow and change, to be always in motion and never still in the constant changes that move and create life in every instant. But it is also mugwort that stands at the gateway of creation and spirit both protecting our vision and giving us safe and balanced passage through into the next step of life.

*'The difficulties of winter and autumn, the heat of summer,*
*spring like the spirit of life, winds and clouds and lightening*
*all these help to make distinctions clear,*
*so the dust-coloured earth may bring forth all it holds in its heart*
*whether ruby or dull stone.'*

Mevlana Jelaluddin Rumi

# HERB ROBERT
## *Geranium Robertianum*

Herb Robert is one of the most charming plants in the garden. It delicately flows in all directions with small pink flowers darting in and out of its greenery. The roots hardly touch the soil and yet it seems to expand with an effortlessness. It gaily dances in and around and under all other plants and loves either sunshine or shade. Her name comes from the Greek word gheranos and means a crane. The Latin erodium means heron. Robertianum probably comes from ruberta and means red. Her flowers are sculpted like a crane's bill and her lightness gives the feeling that the entire plant has the effortlessness of flight. Her flowers were said to have been given their pink colour by Mohammed who left his clothes to dry. The flowers blushed bright pink and red at the sight and have been that colour ever since. Both the flowers and leaves have a strong sharp odour. This odour has earned it the name of stinking bob in parts of England. If one dreams of this wild geranium it means someone will have a change of interests. Herb robert is the sacred plant of the green man of the woods and was used by the Druids to contact the woodland lord himself.

In ancient times herb robert was thought capable of mending fractures and applied to wounds to stop the bleeding. The strong smell of its leaves made it a good insect repellent. It was used as a tonic for blood as it lowers blood sugar levels. Culpepper said it was good for stopping blood in wounds, and good for old ulcers. It was also used as a decoction to help in obstructions of the kidneys and stones. It was used for mouth sores as well as a gargle and for eye irritations. A cloth soaked in an infusion was used for the irritation of skin conditions. The tea is said to be good for peptic ulcers, diarrhoea and internal haemorrhage. In modern day it is used as an antiseptic and wound healer. It is also thought to be effective against stomach ulcers, inflammation of the uterus and may have some potential as a treatment for cancer.

Herb robert is the magical messenger. She knows no boundaries and is in contact with every other plant. She is this wholeness within nature. In healing, every plant can be contacted through her. In this way she is the open gateway of the garden and the keeper of all its plants and riches.

# OAK
## *Quercus*

Oak is considered to be the father of mankind and the Romans believed that man sprang from the oak itself. As Virgil wrote, 'These woods were first the seat of sylvan powers of nymphs and fawns and savage men who took their birth from the trunks of trees and the stubborn oak'. Oaks are simply magnificent. To sit with one's back against a mighty oak is to feel nourished by an energy of strength and wisdom. The roots of the oak extend as far underground as the branches are above the ground gathering the vitality of heaven and earth. Its catkins form in early summer and grow into the acorn that feeds many wild animals of the forest with its soft nut. The oak enriches all around it with shade, shelter and food. For thousands of years it has provided natural cover for the hills and valleys of the earth. Throughout this time the oak has been considered the king of the forest. It can live for hundreds of years and when cut down often throws up shoots that grow into a new tree. Many of the great oaks are known to be over 800 years old. They are often honoured during celebrations and some have become sacred trees where offerings are left in return for blessings. Here lives the royal lord of the forest full of strength, virility and protection. gaining its primal energy from the deep sources of the earth and the vast expanses of the sky. The name of the oak is said to come from the Celtic word, quer meaning fine and cuez, meaning tree.

The oak flowers in the heart of summer and these flowers are often used to strengthen and purify the celebrations of midsummer. The festival of the oak is traditionally celebrated on the 29th of May when the oak and other trees are dressed with presents. It is said the oak's flowers mark the doorway to the close of summer and the opening of winter.

In Roman times the god Jupiter was worshipped in the form of an oak tree. In Greek times the same god called Zeus had his ancient sanctuary in a sacred oak called quercus, the Greek name for the oak. This was said to be an oracle tree which gave prophecies in the rustling of its leaves or in the murmurings of the sacred spring which rose from its roots. It was said a beam of this tree was placed in the ship of the Argonauts to give them advice during their voyage. Zeus disguised as an old man at one point was given hospitality by an elderly couple. They were given one wish and Philomon asked that at death he be turned into an oak tree and his wife into a linden tree so they would never be parted. In the times of the Druids, a Druid was said to be a person of oak knowledge. They would carve a quartered circle on an oak as protection against lightening. Any oak that is struck down by lightening was believed to be very powerful and people would come from miles around to take a talisman from the tree. The oak is said to open the door to knowledge. It is believed that if a dressing from a wound is placed inside a hollow in an oak tree, then the wound will be transferred through the tree into the ground and the wound will be healed. When an oak is cut one should place an acorn near the old tree to provide a new home for its spirit.

The dreaming of an Oak tree is lucky and if there is an acorn growing on it, then it foretells of children who will make their parents proud. It is said carrying a piece of oak protects its bearer from harm and if you catch a falling oak leaf you will have no colds during the winter. Carrying a piece of oak is said to preserve youthfulness and lighting an oak fire in the hearth will draw off an illness in the house. Carrying an acorn is believed to increase fertility and strengthen sexual potency. Planting an acorn in the dark cycle of the moon is said to bring money in the future.

In ancient times the tea of the bark was used for diarrhoea, infections of the digestive tract, liver and bladder problems. Externally the decoction was used for rashes, wounds, burns, and as a gargle for sore throats. The bark is the part of the tree largely used in healing. It was used for haemorrhages and can be substituted for quinine in intermittent fevers. It was useful in chronic diarrhoea and dysentery. Bruised leaves have been used to heal wounds. The powder of acorns made with milk was considered by the ancients to be an antidote to poisonous herbs and medicine. The distilled water of the oak bud was thought to be good internally or externally for inflammation including vaginal infections and as a gargle for sore throats. The bark has also been used to tan leather and to smoke fish.

Today a decoction maybe used as a gargle to treat sore throats and tonsillitis. The bark may also be applied as a wash, lotion or ointment to treat haemorrhoids, anal fissures, small burns, and other skin problems. A decoction of the bark can also be used for diarrhoea, dysentery and powdered bark can be sprinkled on eczema to dry the affected area.

Bach used the oak flowers for despondency, and despair where people struggle on in the face of every difficulty. He describes oak people like the oak tree itself, being able to stand great strain, strong physically, very patient and full of common sense. However there can come a time when the despondency and despair become too much. He describes the positive aspects of oak as being brave people fighting against great difficulties without the loss of hope or slackening of effort, reflecting perseverance, courage and stability under all conditions.

Imagine watching the changes as several hundreds of years pass in all their cycles of rain, wind, snow, sunshine and mists. All around there are animals, flowers, and trees that are born, grow and then pass away in their time. You even see the great rivers change their course and see villages grow into towns and men change their style of clothes. You use and enjoy whatever nature brings knowing this to be the most important part of life. You are the king of the forest because of your centuries of life. Your roots fill the land with this knowledge and wisdom protecting all around you with strength, longevity, and a vast understanding of the world around. The oak absorbs and grows by soaking in the rains and dews on its leaves and directing the life giving liquid to the roots. These roots give the greatest of stability. Its trunk gives a sturdiness that withstands the constantly changing seasons and its limbs span vast distances. The tree simply uses its time to grow thus gaining a vast strength of great wisdom and knowledge.

*'We cannot fathom the mystery of a single flower,*
*Nor is it intended that we should.'*

John Ruskin

# MORNING GLORY
## *Convolvulus*

Morning glory flowers in the fullness of the morning, her bell shaped flowers ringing out this new start. The flowers are like fine trumpets announcing the creation of each day. She then closes by lunchtime to reappear with the next dawn. In the wild, the flowers are often striped with pink, blue or purple. The five petalled flower is like a delicate cup that is able to open wide to the innocent newness and fresh vision that comes with each day. The flower is completely open as if made with the ability to take in all that is around it. It brings beauty to the most derelict places like old fences, crumbling brickwork or concrete walls, with its spiralling vines, heart shaped leaves and old fashioned flowers resembling the skirts of long ball dresses. It always winds in the same direction. In fact if it is rewound in the opposite direction it ceases to grow.

The plant itself is a relative of the sweet potato which is a tuberous rooted bindweed. The sweet potato roots abound in starch and sugar and form a nourishing food. Morning glory strangles anything that it climbs around and because of this it is often a symbol of dangerous obstinacy. Because of the short life of its flowers it is said to represent fleeting joy. The Greek name comes from ips meaning worm and homoios meaning like and expresses its worm like stem that is able to eventually strangle anything it climbs up. The Latin convolulus comes from convolva which means twisted. The species name sepium comes from the Latin sepes which means a hedge. The generic name calystegia comes from the Greek word kalyx meaning a cup and stege meaning a covering.

A tincture of the flowers has been used for headaches, rheumatism and inflamed eyes. It has been used as a purgative but the dosage is difficult and it is no longer used in this way by herbalists. The seeds of the Mexican variety contain a hallucagenic compound and were taken by both the Zapotecs and Aztecs in their ancient rituals. The Iroquois believed that morning glory had the ability to heal or harm and should be picked, stored and used with great care. They considered morning glory to be so powerful that even touching it could cause harm. The Iroquois used the plant, ipomoea pandurata as a remedy for coughs, tuberculosis and other ailments. It was also taken as a decoction with sunflower seeds as a sacrament in spring and autumn rituals. Placing the seeds beneath a pillow is said to stop all nightmares. When it is grown in the garden it is said to bring peace and happiness. The root is said to bring protection, love and success. It is also said that if the root is anointed with oil and placed in a green sachet it can be carried to attract money and to stop depression.

Imagine an early morning when the mist is hanging heavily on the gardens. Gradually the sun seeps through the clouds and the mist lifts. Suddenly the garden is fresh and bright. You are able to see details and life in the garden that you were never aware of before. Suddenly your vision has been cleared like washing a dusty window in an attic room and you are able to see the world in brilliant detail. Sometimes we need to wipe clean the mist and dust on the window first, as well as change and let go of the unuseful things of the past, before we can open the window wide and really take in the freshness of each moment in life. If not, what is there is still covered in old ideas and our mind is still full of unresolved thoughts. But when we are able to face the world with fresh innocence and curiosity, then opening the window can bring a fresh understanding and inspiration to what is possible in life. We can see the vitality in all that we do and in all the life that surrounds us. Here is the freshness of the early morning when the promise of the new day is at its fullest.

Here it is as though every tree, flower and plant sparkles with life. Each person we meet suddenly has a special quality of their own. We can see the beauty in all around us and new possibilities emerge out of this wonder. We are suddenly awake with fresh spring vision and can see the heavenly palaces overhead. This open vision is the spirit of morning glory.

*'A morning-glory at my window satisfies me more
than the metaphysics of books.'*

Walt Whitman

*'You are a ruby embedded in granite.
How long will you pretend it isn't true?
We can see it in your eyes.
Come to the root of the root of your Self.'*

Mevlana Jelalludin Rumi

# SELF HEAL
## *Prunella Vulgaris*

For centuries, self heal and the related species bugle, have been thought to possess great curative powers. Culpepper went so far as to say that it was a plant one would fall in love with. Self heal and bugle are small plants with shiny oval leaves. The flowers grow on a single stalk and resemble long bells with two lips or cones or ears or tiny orchids one on top of the other. They are deep blue like the night sky at dusk They appear in the early spring and last until midsummer. They are always in clusters of plants and have a richness of energy like a revitalizing spring around them. One can almost see the fairies in amongst the leaves.

The name bugle comes from the dark, lustrous, long beads which were once sown into clothes as ornaments. Ajuga comes from the Latin abija meaning to drive away, for the plants were thought to drive away various forms of disease. Self heal's name prunella comes from the German 'die breuen'. It was called that because of its ability to cure inflammation of the mouth.

Gerard wrote that there is not a better wound herb in the world. Culpepper said 'If the virtues of it make you fall in love with it (as they will if you be wise), keep a syrup of it to take inwardly and an ointment and plaster of it to use outwardly, always by you'. He said it is effective for any inward or outward wound whether new or old. In those times it was used for gangrene. It was also used for sores in the mouth and gums as well as sores in the secret parts of men and women. It was said to help when someone drank too much! A juice mixed with oil of roses helped to remove headaches. An infusion was used in arresting haemorrhages as well as for coughs, allaying irritation. It equalizes the circulation and is a mild narcotic. It is good for green wounds and closes them together. In the seventeenth century it was commonly put into decoctions for wounds and it was said that he who has bugle or self heal will not need the surgeon.

In modern times self heal has been shown to have a mildly dilating effect on the blood vessels and helps to lower blood pressure. It also has a strong antibiotic effect on infections both internally and externally. For these reasons it is used as a wound herb. It is also sometimes taken to reduce internal bleeding and as a gargle to treat sore throats. It is also used for vaginal discharge and haemorrhoids.

Imagine having no joy, no laughter, no hope, and a deep emptiness inside. Everything seems grey and dull. There are no flowers in the world to brighten the fields with colours. There is no ice-cream or chocolate to have as a special treat at the end of a hard day. The world is a place where no one ever smiles or lends a hand when someone needs it. This is indeed a grey world where the excitement and inspiration has gone out of life. Then imagine all of these things coming back into life. There is a meal with beautifully cooked food, polished glasses and friends full of laughter and love. Children are playing and sharing games. Suddenly there are two eagles with their young soaring over head. You sit on a veranda overlooking beautiful gardens in which to recover your warmth, joy, hope, reserves and resources. This is self heal's great ability to bring back the spirit of life when illness has been long, when suffering has been great and when hope has been lost.

*'If all the plants and beasts were gone,*
*we would die from loneliness of spirit,*
*for whatever happens to the plants and beasts happens to us.*
*All things are connected.*
*Whatever befalls the earth befalls the sons of the earth.'*

Chief Seattle

*'The garden of love is green without limit*
*And yields many fruits other than sorrow or joy,*
*Love is beyond either condition... it is always fresh.'*

Mevlana Jelaluddin Rumi

# CHICORY
## *Cichorium Intybus*

Chicory is filled with sky blue flowers from the height of summer until the autumn. To see a full field of chicory is like being in heaven. The large cornflowers fill the delicate slightly hairy green stems with a lightness and charm that brings hope and warmth to the heart and spirit. The flowers themselves only last a few hours. They open with the sun and by midday have closed again. They then rebloom the next day. It is said Linnaeus used them for keeping the time. This fleeting nature reminds us of the transient nature of both time and of the seasons. The leaves themselves always are aligned with the north. It has a thick root that gives a milky substance when it is opened.

The Arabs boiled the roots for food and its name is thought to come from the Arab word Chiouryeh. The name also comes from the Latin succurrere meaning to run under because of the depth that the roots penetrate. The root was eaten in ancient Egypt as a roasted vegetable, by the Israelites on the passover with lamb, and by the Romans as a boiled vegetable. In ancient times it was said that the juice of chicory rubbed all over the body would obtain favours from an important person. It was believed that chicory made the carrier invisible and if it was gathered at noon on midsummer's day, with a golden knife, in silence, it could open all locks held against a person. It was carried to remove all obstacles in life. The Celts believed that if it was carried it would remove all difficulties in your path through life, promote frugality and help to forget a lost love. It was also used as a herb of divination to wash wands, crystal balls and the third eye.

It is said that the beautiful blue flowers come from the eyes of a weeping girl crying for her lover who never returned. There is also a German legend about a girl waiting for the return of her lover. When he did not return she fell by the roadside and died. The blue flowers of chicory sprang up on the spot where she lay.

Culpepper said that chicory or what he called succory is effective for sore eyes that are inflamed and for nursing breasts that are pained with too much milk. A handful of leaves boiled in wine was good for the liver, gallbladder and spleen and to help jaundice and the kidneys. The bruised leaves could help with swellings and skin eruptions. The distilled water was good for passions of the heart, headache and for the stomach. The decoction has been used to treat liver disorders, gallstones, kidney stones and for urinary inflammations. The richness of the leaves in calcium, copper and iron help with jaundice and difficulties with the spleen and the liver as well as cleansing the digestion and treating eczema and boils and other skin problems. Poultices are said to help reduce inflammation.

Bach used chicory when love was blocked in its outward flow. It is when the individual has become congested mentally and physically because the outward love they could give has become a grasping possessiveness. In this way the person becomes over-possessive of others and may want to control and direct the lives of others that are close to him. As Bach says such a person may even invoke an illness to keep people waiting on him and sympathizing with him. The positive aspect is when one is truly selfless in their care and concern for others. The person then becomes someone who can give unceasingly and without the slightest thought of a return.

In modern times chicory root is dried and ground and then added to coffee. It is said it corrects the excitation caused by coffee. The root is laxative and diuretic and can be effective for liver complaints such as jaundice and for rheumatism. It stimulates the flow of bile and helps with digestion. The young leaves can be eaten in salads usually after being blanched to remove the bitter taste. The roots are cooked as a vegetable being boiled and eaten with butter like parsnips. The flowers are used to decorate salads and cakes. It is a mild bitter tonic for the liver and digestive tract. The root is like dandelion root and supports the action of the stomach and liver and cleanses the urinary tract. It is also taken for rheumatic conditions and gout, and as a mild laxative. An infusion of the leaves aids the digestion.

Imagine a warm safe place where your heart is protected from the bruises, rejections and losses in life. It is a warm nurturing place to return to when life has been harsh and rough and needs a softer place to refind the love, joy, calm and hope that gives each day enormous pleasure. It is like holding a warm and adoring cat in your arms on a pleasant sunny day. Here the blue flowers of chicory wash away the bruises and hurts like refreshing waters protecting the new skin until it is healed enough to face the world again with warmth. Here we can become courageous enough to again love what comes.

*'Just as the heart becomes carefree in a place of green growing plants, goodwill and kindness are born when our souls enter happiness.'*

Mevlana Jelaluddin Rumi

# AGRIMONY
## *Agrimonia Eupatoria*

Agrimony is a graceful delight of the garden with an odour of apricots on its flowers and a sweet scent on its roots. The seeds cling to the garments of passers by as if desirous of accompanying them. A spring drink is sometimes made with the leaves for bringing the senses alive to the fragrances of all the newly growing plants and their virtues. The flowers are a beautiful rich ripe yellow with pretty purple red or pale yellow centres. They grow up a central stalk. These long flower spikes of agrimony have caused the name of church steeples to be given the plant. There is a deep richness to everything about agrimony. It is as though she has been painted in thick oils dripping with vitality. The flowers grows out of a rossette of leaves that are a rich green deeply veined with serrated edges.

Its name comes from agremone which means white speck on the eye and reflects the ancient belief that it could cure all eye disorders including cataracts. The name eupatoria comes from the name of the King of Pontus, Mithridates Eupator in northern Turkey, who was said to have discovered the curative properties of the plant. He had a profound knowledge of plant lore. Gerard says it was once called philanthropos either because of its beneficent and valuable properties, or because of the way that seeds cling to the garments of passers-by. It was one of the common plants in medieval monasteries and was used to treat open wounds and stomach problems. Agrimony was said to repel all forms of negative energy that would lead to depression, lethargy or physical and spiritual energy drain. It was used to clean the house, temples and sacred sites of any negative energy. Agrimony wine was drunk in ritual ceremonies. In an old English manuscript it was said that if it be laid under a man's head, he shall sleep as though dead and not awake until it is taken from under his head.

The Anglo-Saxons called it garclive and said it would heal wounds, snake bites and warts. In the time of Chaucer it was used with mugwort to heal all wounds and a bad back. It was one of the ingredients for the arquebusade water used for wounds, sprains and bruises. Culpepper said that agrimony draweth forth thorns and splinters of wood, nails, or any other such thing gotten into the flesh. He said it helps clean the liver and bowels and heals all inward wounds, bruises, hurts and other distempers. He goes on to say that drunk in wine it was good against the bites of serpents, cleaning the urine, helping with colic and cleaning the lungs. Mixed with old swine's grease it helped old sores, cancers and ulcers. It was a remedy for jaundice and giving a tonic to the system and promoting the assimilation of food. It was also said to strengthen parts out of joint.

Bach says of an agrimony type that on the surface it is someone who appears to be very cheerful and is pleasurable to be with. However the person wears the mask of carefreeness superficially, while deep within himself he is a severely tortured person. He is peace loving and distressed by quarrels and arguments. He goes on to say that they are people who make light of their troubles during the day but at night are often restless with churning thoughts. They seek companionship in order to escape from and to forget their worries. They can resort to alcohol or drugs to dull the mental torture which they are experiencing. The positive side comes when the person can truly laugh at their own worries because they can see the unimportance. They then become genuine optimists and peacemakers.

In modern times agrimony is used for coughs, skin eruptions, and cystitis. It is helpful as a tonic and blood cleanser for sore throats, and mouth inflammations. The bruised leaves can be made into a poultice to ease arthritic and rheumatic joints. The cooled infusion can also be used as an eye bath. An agrimony herb pillow gives restful sleep. Agrimony has long been used to heal wounds because of its ability to staunch bleeding and encourage clotting. It can be used to help diarrhea and is a gentle tonic for the digestion. It can also be used for urinary incontinence, kidney stones and sore throats.

Imagine feeling empty, alone, and that something is missing in life. For some reason there is no sparkle to each day, no inspiration. Life seems to have lost its lustre. Everything seems routine and without variation. Then imagine having a wonderful massage where suddenly your body feels good. Then you are fed on the harvest foods of the late summer. You are dressed in warm, soft clothing. The sunrise is one of the most beautiful you have ever seen. Everyone you meet is warm and friendly and wants to know how you are and what you are doing with genuine concern. Here your spirit is refreshed and you are able to see the world in richer hues.

Suddenly the gateway opens into the gardens of the great palace. You watch the slow running stream as the wild birds sing. Here you are served drinks of wild exotic tastes and eat the delicacies of the inner kingdom. Imagine sitting in the magical inner gardens of this great palace. You rest by the fountains watching the water sparkle in sunlight. As you pass the roses each opens sharing its delightful scent. There are beds of irises of every colour in the rainbow. You walk through walls full of honeysuckle and jasmine. Suddenly there are fields of cornflowers, poppies and chicory. The sky is blue with delightfully shaped clouds. The birds chatter and sing. It is this refreshment and reawakening that agrimony brings to the spirit, gently enticing it back to the full enjoyment of what life can bring to the heart and all its senses.

*'What a desolate place would a world without flowers!*
*It would be a face without a smile,*
*a feast without a welcome.'*

Clara Balfour

# BROOM
## *Cytisus Scoparius*

Broom is glorious in the late spring. It sends streams of bright yellow lantern like flowers cascading down the hillside. They give out a fragrant sweet scent. The bees fill their baskets on their hind legs with deep rich yellow pollen that the flowers shower on them in great abundance. The plant has slightly intoxicating properties and shepherds are aware that when their sheep eat the tops they become slightly drunk and then become sleepily relaxed. The effect soon passes. Broom is full of abundance. For the eyes its flowers are delicate and full, covering branch after branch with whole streams of blossoms. Its pollen dusts the air with sweetness. Its roots hold even the sandiest soil together making it a perfect sheltering place for seaside growth and to hold the earth together on steep slopes. It is this abundance of magnificent yellow that takes the breath away in spring. Heather's purple flowers do the same thing in the fall.

The broom has long been a plant of love in many folk legends. One thirteenth century legend tells of a wife asking the being in the broom to teach her how to have her husband truly love her. The broom replies that if her tongue be still she shall have her will. Sacred grounds were cleared with broom before ceremonies. It was said that to raise the winds broom should be thrown into the air and to calm the winds the broom should be burnt and the ashes buried. It is believed that if broom is abundant in flowers then the grain harvest will be exceptional. It can be placed in the house for protection and carried to help with psychic powers.

Its English name comes from using its branches for making brooms, basketwork, thatching and fencing. Its shoots were also used for making paper or cloth in the same way flax was used. Its original Greek name sarothammus means to sweep and a shrub. The Latin name scopariuos comes from scopa meaning a besom. The generic name cytisus seems to be a corruption of the name of a Greek island Cythnus where broom abounded. Geoffrey of Anjou was said to have thrust a branch into his helmet going into battle and said, 'This golden plant, rooted firmly amid rock, yet upholding what is ready to fall, shall be my cognizance'. It is also on the great seal of Richard I. The

Plantagetnet kings of England are so named because of their adoption of the spring of broom (in Latin called plantagenista) as a heraldic device. The young buds and tips were gathered and placed in pickle or salt and then washed or boiled to be eaten in salads like capers. It has been carried at weddings by the guests to bring happiness to the marrying couple.

Gerard said it was good to drink the distilled water of broom against suffering and diseases. Broom wine was said to help in the healing of diseases. He goes on to say that the decoction of the twigs and tops of the broom clean and open the liver, milt and kidneys. Culpepper thought that broom was good for the dropsy, black jaundice, gout, sciatica and various pains of the hips and joints. A decoction of broom was also used for bladder and kidney affections.

Today broom can be used for irregular, fast heartbeats. The plant acts on the electrical conductivity of the heart slowing and regulating the impulses. It also stimulates urine production and counteracts fluid retention. It has been used to prevent blood loss after childbirth because of its ability to cause the muscles of the uterus to contract.

One day an ordinary piece of clay lay in the sunshine wondering who it was. The rest of the clay around it thought it was silly to think about it be being more than just clay. However it continued to feel deep inside it was something more than just this piece of earth. One morning a potter came and spent some time looking at the earth. He looked at all the colours and pick up several handfuls of clay. The small piece of clay was filled with a yearning that he would be picked up as well. The man walked over and studied his colour and with great gentleness took the piece of clay in his hand holding it up to the sun to see all the colours and texture in its form. The potter put the piece in his bag and took it home. The next day he moistened the clay with water and the piece of clay felt alive as if something very special was about to happen. The man shaped the clay into a ball and placed it on his wheel. He sent it spinning and began shaping the raw clay into a beautiful bowl. When he was happy with the shape he placed the bowl out in the sun to dry. The clay felt elegant and began to realize it was becoming something very special.

Several days passed and the potter then began to paint the bowl with special colours and patterns. He next put wood into the kiln until it was just the right temperature. He then gently placed the bowl in the kiln. The bowl was cooked for hours until all the glaze had melted and became a beautiful design. The pot was slowly cooled in the open air. It was then brought into the house of the potter and used to hold the main dishes that were wonderfully prepared by the potter's wife. The bowl lasted centuries and is still used today. The piece of clay was finally able to be who it was. By gracious and skilled hands, and the fire of the kiln it had been transformed into its own special beauty.

Broom lightens our load like sweeping the room clear of all its dust and debris. Here we can be moistened, shaped and fired in the kiln so that the rough interior becomes a vessel of beauty. In this way we can find the rich seal of who we are and can be given the warmth and fire to change. It is here that life takes a new turning and we find ourselves moving forward on fresh breezes. When we become the beauty of who we are, the way becomes more joyful, easier and full of elegance. Broom enables the dullness of our being to blossom into brightness like a polished mirror where our eyes smile with delight. We allow things to come to us. Life suddenly has a purpose and passes in harmony and delightful surprises.

*'I have banished all worldly care from my garden,*
*It is an innocent and open place.'*

Hsien Ling-Yun

# SAGE
## *Salvia*

Sage flowers are shaped like the most wonderful of exotic birds or tiny orchids. The smell is a strong fragrant odour. The leaves are soft and muted greens that are velvety to the touch and when rubbed on the skin take away the sting of insects as well as the sting of the nettle. The plant is sturdy and strong producing its wonderful flowers at the height of the summer. The tea is wonderfully scented and tastes fresh and fortifying. The leaves have been used to flavour meat and fish dishes, eggs and salads. They are a favourite stuffing for all kinds of birds including the traditional turkey. The plant itself is wild and grows in even the most sparse conditions supplying the bees with a strong flavoured nectar. The Germans infused it with elder flowers and added it to wine to produce what was called a muscatel sage. At times it was substituted for hops in beer and was said to make the beer exhilarating. However if too much was drunk it could result in severe headaches.

Its Latin name salvia comes from salvere which means to be saved and implies health. The wild sage is called clary sage which comes from clarus which means to clear. The specific name offisinalis means that the sage was recognized as a medicinal plant. In the middle ages it was said that 'why should a man die if he had sage in his garden?' It was thought the plant would thrive or wither just as the owner's business prospered or failed. Another saying about sage was that the wife would rule if the sage grew vigorously in the garden. Sage was believed to give a long life and it was said that he who eats sage in the month of May will live well into old age. In France it was believed that sage helped to mitigate grief. It was also believed to help the nerves, palsy and to put fevers to flight. Sage has been used as a substitute for tea and for improving the taste of cheeses. Wild Mexican sage seeds are used as a food and called chia. In the seventeenth century the Chinese traded tea for sage and three chests of tea were exchanged for one chest of sage.

It has been used to purify temples by the Greeks and Romans. Even Solomon used it for this purpose. The Native Americans also use sage for purification, healing and cleansing. Carrying sage is said to bring wisdom. Placing the leaves under a pillow is thought to encourage prophetic dreams. It was believed that the seeds beaten into a powder and drunk with wine would produce lust. If you want to make a wish come true you should write on a sage leaf and hide it under your pillow. If you dream of what you desire then the wish will be fulfilled. Sage leaves are carried to promote wisdom and healing. It is said that sage eaten every day will bring long life. Italian people eat sage as a preservative of health placing the leaves between bread and butter.

Sage was one of the Roman's sacred herbs and they believed it benefited most illnesses. The priest would ritually collect the plant by dressing in a white tunic, after having ritually bathed. He would be barefooted and use a knife that was not made of metal. The plant was offered bread and wine as a thank you. Barren women were recommended to take sage with a pinch of salt for four days before intercourse to become pregnant.

Gerard said that sage was good for the head and brain and quickened the senses and memory. He believed that it strengthened the sinews and took away trembling. He felt it was good against snake bite. Sage tea is good for fevers and in nervous excitement. It can also be used as a stimulant for the stomach and nervous system. The leaves are used for sprains and bruises. Culpepper says that it brings on menstruation and expels a dead child, as well as stopping the bleeding of a wound and cleaning ulcers and sores. Toasted seeds help with pains in the head and joints and with the lowness of the spirit causing lethargy. The juice helps with hoarseness and cough and if drunk with vinegar it was thought to be good for the plague. Put into a bath it warms cold joints and soothes cramps. An infusion is useful for diarrhoea, depression, rheumatism, anaemia, menstrual problems, migraine, lowering fevers, indigestion, coughs and colds. Externally it has been used as a wash for skin problems, wounds, scabs and insect bites and stings. It is said to darken greying hair. Smoking the leaves is said to help asthma. The fresh leaves can be rubbed into teeth to whiten them.

In modern times sage has been found to be an excellent remedy for sore throats, poor digestion and irregular menstruation. It is used for canker sores and sore gums. It can also be used for mild diarrhoea. It both calms and stimulates the nervous system. It encourages a better flow of blood and helps in light or irregular menstruation as well as helping hot flashes in the menopause. It is included in herbal smoking mixtures for asthma. Fresh leaves can be rubbed on stings or bites.

One day there was a branch on the ancient willow tree just waiting for something exciting to happen to it. Suddenly three boys came through the wilderness. Two of the boys already had sticks and the third boy came and decided this branch was just what he needed. He carefully cut the branch and admired its curve and flexibility. The boys found a warm place in the open field just outside the woods and carefully stripped the branches of their outer coverings. They then left them in the sun to dry while they had lunch. After eating they skillfully made a small hole at each end of the sticks and placed a string of nettle fibers through the holes. They painted the wood and gave it a name. The willow was called straight and true. The boys then made arrows and tested out the bows. Straight and true sent arrows flying further and straighter than the others. It was very proud to be a strong hunting bow and helped kill many animals.

Sage is the warrior plant that gives strength and courage to vision and purpose in life. Here is the push forward into redoing what is necessary to bring about changes. Here one can look around the corner of what is fearful, let go of what is habituary, move with the courage of doing things alone, and put the warmth of the feelings of the heart into action. In this way we become refreshed by life and it in turn gives us new experiences and delights. There is no holding back with sage. It gives a leap into new directions with a fullness of purpose and the strength of firmly being able to stand on the ground in order to take the next step forward. Here we can fly straight and true like an arrow to the very centre of our goals.

*'Even if I knew certainly the world would end tomorrow
I would plant an apple tree today.'*

Martin Luther

# CORNFLOWER
## *Centaurea Cyanus*

Cornflowers rippling together in fields in the summer with their beautiful blue flowers of delicate soft petal is like seeing a fresh sea or cloudless sky in the heart of the earth herself. This blue is in star like blossoms that makes us sigh with wonder. The stalks are long and slender with delicate leaves supporting the single flower of beauty that blossoms at the top. When reaping was done by hand these delicate looking stems could blunt the reaper's sickle. The seeds that form are like tiny golden stars waiting to be scattered to once again recreate this beauty.

The Latin name centaurea comes from an ancient Greek legend. Chiron the centaur was wounded in the foot by Hercules with poisonous arrows. There was a field of cornflowers nearby who told Chiron to cover the wound with their flowers. It healed the wound and Chiron went on to discover the healing properties of all the plants around him. This wisdom he taught to whoever needed it. The flower was called centaurea after him. Another legend tells of a young boy called Cyanus who worshipped Flora the goddess of plants. He would always gather blue flowers for her and leave them in the forest for her to find. One day he was found dead in the place where he normally gathered the flowers. Flora turned him into a blue cornflower in honour of his love for flowers and his sensitivity to her.

In the olden days if a girl wore a cornflower it was said to mean that she was available for marriage. If the girl hid a cornflower under her apron she would have the bachelor of her choice. She could also ask the flower directly about love by saying, now gentle flower, I pray thee tell, if my love loves me and loves me well. Some sign would be sure to come very soon afterwards. It was said that if a young man put a cornflower in his pocket and he was in love, then if the cornflower lived he should marry but if it died then he should find another sweetheart. The cornflower is said to represent the gifts of the harvest mother for bringing forth life. It was often used by the Druids (either as a concoction or as incense) to experience clairvoyant sight. The dried petals are used by perfumers for giving colour to potpourri. The juice of the petals makes a good blue ink. It is also used as a very fine watercolour. It can dye linen a fine blue colour, but it is not permanent. The petals impart a beautiful blue colour to tea.

A water distilled from the petals was used as a remedy for weak eyes earning it the French name of casselunettes which means to break glasses. Culpepper said that water distilled from the plant is good for bruises caused by a fall or to heal a broken vein. He suggested that used with plantain and horsetail it would be a remedy against the poison of the scorpion. He goes on to say that the seeds or leaves taken in wine is good against the plague and infectious diseases. The juice put into a fresh or green wound helps to heal it. It can also be used for dyspepsia and as an eye lotion. The fifteenth century herbalist, Mattioli held the belief that cornflower's deep blue colour symbolized healthy eyes and hence it became a treatment for eye ailments.

Today it is largely used in bath preparations or in compressions to treat wounds or skin ulcers. It is one of the best herbs for hay fever. A mild infusion can be used to bath the eyes to reduce itchiness. As a tea it is good for digestive disorders. The petals are taken as a bitter tonic and stimulant to improve the digestion and to support the liver while improving resistance to infection. A decoction of the leaves is used to treat rheumatic complaints.

Imagine visiting a healing spring deep in the mountains. Here you meet the spirit of the spring who is a beautiful being. Suddenly you are full of old hurts, bruises, fears, and anxieties. Gently she takes her blue water and slowly washes away the bruises, then the hurts, then the fears and at last the anxieties. You are clean and fresh again. You imagine how to forgive the hurts, how to face the fears and how to calm the anxieties. She give you a fresh cup of water to drink and you feel a lightness and wealth of energy bubble up inside of you. You can hear the spring waters gurgling and laughing beside you. You can feel the refreshing waters moving throughout your veins clearing your sight and senses. Suddenly life take on a refreshing quality.

Cornflower is like the blue sky on a sunny summer's afternoon, calm and tranquil. It is the blue sea with gentle breezes moving the sails without effort. It is a blue pool full of silent brightly coloured fishes. Cornflower is full of blueness to calm our fears, sooth our bruises and ease our anxieties.

*'It is good to be alone in a garden at dawn or dark*
*so that all its shy presence may haunt you*
*and possess you in a reverie of suspended thought.'*

James Douglas

# POPPY
## *Papaver Rhoeas*

Poppy is a flower of purest silk in all its elegance. To watch a poppy open is like unfolding the most precious treasure wrapped in red silk cloth. The green head slowly opens and the wrinkled red petals seem to grow into the most impossible size until they unfold and straighten themselves out on the breezes revealing the rich deep dark chocolate centre of nectar and pollen. Here is a scarlet cup of flowing silk the colour of burning coal that seems to fall from the heavenly altars above. It is like the magician of the garden suddenly appearing where it pleases and then the next year suddenly flowering somewhere entirely different. This fantastic extravagant scarlet flower in ancient times was called the red rose of Ceres.

The Romans believed the flower was raised by Ceres, the corn goddess who always held both the poppy and the cornflower in her embrace. It was the Roman god of sleep who fashioned crowns of poppies to place on the heads of those he wanted to sleep. It is said that Ceres at one time was very tired and neglectful of her crops so the God of Sleep created the poppy to induce her to rest. Her strength returned and the harvest was plentiful. When the goddess Demeter finally sat down during her search for her lost daughter Persephone, the gods caused poppies to grow at her feet. Here she rested for nine days and nights and then discovered her daughter was in the underworld of Hades. The poppy became a symbol of spring, the time when her daughter was once again allowed on earth knowing she would have to descend again in the fall.

The name papaver comes from the Latin word pappa which means breast referring to the milky white fluid that comes out when the ripening capsule is broken. In the opium poppy this is what is made into opium. Rhoeas comes from the Greek word rho and means red. It also comes from the Latin rhoes meaning a falling or flow which refers to the fragile way the petal can easily come off.

The poppy is a plant of fertility, abundance and sacrifice, symbolizing the flowering of each spring and the death of autumn. The Romans wove the poppies into garlands and offered them in rituals to ensure fertility of the crops. It was said that poppies must not be picked for fear of evoking storms.

The Egyptians felt the poppy represented blood and new life. The Assyrians called the poppy the daughter of the fields and it was believed that the corn crop would be improved if there were poppies in the field. The fragrance of the flower is faint but rich and sweet like opium. The rich red silk petals are fragile and inspire the soft intimate wonders within our own hearts. Poppy seeda are used to decorate cakes and breads. Each plant has the capacity to produce around 17,000 seeds. The seeds and flowers were used in mixtures to aid sleep. The oil can be used instead of olive oil. The green leaves are eaten in salads or cooked as a vegetable. The petals are traditionally gathered in cloth pouches hung around the neck. They are then made into a syrup that is used for coughs or made into a watercolour or ink.

Carrying poppy seeds is suppose to promote fertility and to attract luck and money. At one time the seed heads were gilded with gold and worn as talismans to bring wealth. It is said if you wish to know the answer to a question write it in blue ink on white paper and place it inside a poppy seed pod and put it under your pillow. The answer will appear in a dream. The seeds when added to food was said to induce love. It is said that if one soaked poppy seeds in wine for fifteen days and then drank the wine while fasting for five days the person could then make themselves invisible at will. If poppy seeds were added to food it was said it would help a woman become pregnant. A harvest loaf decorated with poppy seeds is said to bring blessings to the cycles of the year.

Culpepper says of the poppy that the syrup made of the seeds is useful to give sleep and rest to invalids. The syrup made from the seeds and flowers is also of help with catarrhs, colds, hoarseness, consumption, and loss of voice. A tea made from the petals will help with asthma, bronchitis, catarrh, whooping cough and angina. The Irish herbalist, K'Eogh said the poppy had a cooling and refreshing nature. A decoction of five or six heads in wine is said to bring relief to pain and induce sleep. The bruised leaves have also been used for boils, hot ulcers and burning fevers. In recent history the poppy is used mainly as a mild pain reliever and as a treatment for irritable coughs and nervous overactivity. It is also used for insomnia, nervous irritability, coughs and asthma. It is usually given as a syrup or in wine.

Poppy is pure passion. It is the love a mother has for its child that is overwhelmingly full of great joy. It is how the heart feels when a two year old child smiles with adoring love. It is the passion one feels when in love, where all meetings and conversations are full of pleasure and almost unbearable desire. It is the total involvement in writing or painting that brings something alive on the paper. It is seeing the most wonderful sunset and remembering the friends who have died and how they still live in the memories of the heart. It is knowing there is something greater guiding what happens. It is the richness of knowing we are a part of something greater and letting our hearts follow that pathway. Poppy awakens our desires like a rosy red sunrise full of promise and reminds us of all the love we have inside. Imagine a lying in a field of poppies in the warm May sunshine. Imagine hands of silk caressing your skin with warmth bringing laughter and joy. Imagine Persephone herself appearing and running into the arms of her mother Demeter. These are the fires that poppy awakens with its spirit.

*'Come to the orchard in spring.*
*There is light and wine, and sweethearts*
*in the pomegranate flowers.'*

Mevelana Jelaluddin Rumi

# HAREBELL
## *Campanula Rotundifolia*

Harebells are the most delicate of flowers. They flower in the midsummer with the most delicate soft green stems that have the slenderest of leaves. The bells that hang down are a soft blue or violet and move with the slightest breezes. Harebells were cultivated by ancient people both for the plant as well as the root. The plant can be boiled like young asparagus and eaten with a nob of butter. The flowers and leaves can be used in salads. The leaves have a spinach like flavour. The root which was called a rampion gave the harebell the common name of bell rampion. The name rapanculus comes from the Latin word rapa and means a turnip for the roots could be boiled and roasted in the same way. Campanula comes from the Latin and means to be bell like. In the middle ages it was gathered and boiled like a parsnip and then was roasted or eaten with a sauce. The root is sweetish in flavour. Sometimes the young roots are eaten raw in vinegar or eaten in salads grated along with the young leaves and flowers. There are tales of harebells being found in forests and when lifted up, underneath there are staircases leading to magic places and palaces within the earth. They were said to grow in magician's gardens for this reason.

Gerard says that the bell flowers are good for all inflammations of the mouth and throat. It is also said that the distilled water of bell flowers is excellent for the complexion and makes the face very splendid.

Diamonds when rough are like ordinary stones, but when they are cut and polished they shine and reflect rainbow colours. The fine angles of the flowers of harebell are cut with this precision. Here is a refined precision that brings delicate beauty. Within everyone is the ability to grow, change and refine talents and abilities so they better serve what life can be. The roughness is gradually refined into a fine flower that has only one sweet fragrance. Here is our essence and inner ability to become the specialness of who we are. The spirit of harebell is like a gateway into that fragrance. It is like finding our inner seal or stamp that gives inspiration to our life. From this fresh flower comes the ability to move forward with pride and approval whether we become a brilliant hard diamond smoothly polished or a delicate soft flower perfectly crafted. Here is our true spirit showing the way through the gate of life.

# WILD ROSE
## *Rosa Canina*

Wild rose is a flower of love. It has simple petals that are the most sweetly scented of all roses. The petals often have a delicate blush of pink and their centres are always golden. The leaves shine with green and the woody stems are protected with thorns. Roses have been cultivated for centuries to adorn all occasions from one's first love to death. It is said its birth place was in ancient Persia where roses were called the flower of spirit. The Romans adorned their wines, tables, food, baths and houses with roses. Even in winter they would float rose petals in their wine. The rose in Greek legend was said to have sprung from the blood of Adonis the lover of Aphrodite. It is a flower of beauty, love, poetry and dedicated to Venus.

Another story says it was made as the flower of love. It was created by Chloris the goddess of flowers out of the body of a lifeless nymph. She asked the help of Aphrodite the goddess of love who gave the flower its beauty. Dionysus, the god of wine added nectar to the flower which gave it a sweet scent. The three graces gave it charm, brightness and joy. The west wind, Zephyr then blew away all the clouds so the sun god Apollo could shine with all his might and make the flower bloom. This is how the rose was born and become the queen of the flowers.

Medieval knights wore embroidered roses on their sleeves to symbolize that gentleness should go with courage and that beauty should be the true reward of valour. Rosaries were originally strings of beads made from pressed petals. The word Rosa comes from the Greek word rodon and means red which was the crimson colour of the early cultivated roses. There are over 10,000 known roses in cultivation today.

The story of rose oil comes from the far east. Its discovery happened at the wedding of the princess Nour-Djihan with the Emperor Kjihanguyr. For the reception the canal was filled with rose water. As the couple were rowing after the wedding the princess noticed that the oil had separated from the water in the hot sunlight. As she skimmed this off the canal water, she was delighted to smell the wonderful scent it gave. Afterwards it was this oil that was made into delicate perfumes. For the alchemist the rose symbolizes divine or mystic love. It is thought the alchemist and physician Avicenna was the first person to make distilled flower essences and rose water. It is said if one suspends a rose over the dinner table then all confidences were to be taken with the heart and held to be sacred.

Roses have been used in love potions for centuries. Rose water added to the bath is said to bring love. Rose hips strung together and worn are said to attract love. Women used to take three green rose leaves and name each one of their lovers on the leaves. The one that stayed green the longest was said to indicate their true love. A tea of rosebuds drunk before sleep was said to bring prophetic dreams. When roses are carried they are said to protect and encourage the approach of love. Rose petals sprinkled around the house are said to calm upheaval and stress. Roses planted in the garden attract fairies.

During the middle ages and into the renaissance, the rose was esteemed as a remedy for depression. Gerard said that distilled rose water was good for strengthening the heart and refreshing the spirit as well as for all things that needed a gentle cooling. He went on to say that the sweet and pleasant odour helped to relieve pain and brought sleep. Culpepper lists many uses of the rose and said if he would write all the uses it would swell his book too large. It was used in that time for infection including jaundice and joint aches. Sugared rose petals were thought to be good for swooning, tremblings of the heart, promoting digestion and to strengthen the heart and spirit. Honey added to roses was thought to be good for throat problems. Rose water was thought to refresh the body and bring the spirits back. It was also used as an eye lotion. The oil of roses was used for inflammations and swellings. The leaves were used internally or externally to cool and bind. When the petals were put into wine it was said to be good for headaches, pains in the eyes, ears, throat and gums. The rose hips which are full of vitamin C were dipped in sugar and eaten as a sweet or used in jams, syrups, and tarts. They make a delicate wine for colds and the conserve was said to help consumptive persons. Both are used for coughs and colds. The name hip comes from the Anglo-Saxon word hiope which means flask shaped.

Bach in his flower remedies says that the wild rose is for people who have become resigned to their illnesses or uncongenial work or to their monotonous lives. They are people who don't seem to be able to enjoy the simple pleasures of life and seem to go through life without joy or pleasure.

They seem resigned and apathetic. The positive side is people who have a lively interest in all that is happening around them and this interest and vitality attracts excellent conditions in their lives where they are able to enjoy friends, happiness and good health.

Roses have been used to help treat chest problems for centuries and still today are used for that purpose. The hips have high levels of vitamins that are readily absorbed by the body when fresh and because of this are used to make a nourishing syrup for young children. Roses reduce thirst, alleviate gastric inflammation and are a mild diuretic. In aromatherapy roses are used as a mild sedative, anti-depressant and anti-inflammatory. To have a good night's sleep one should wash the face with rose water and scatter petals around the room. Rose water is used for conjunctivitis and for dry inflamed sensitive skin. The rose is the symbol of divine love that creates all things on earth with the light of its loving embrace.

English rose gardens are some of the most enchanting places. The smells are delightful and the over abundance of roses is an amazing feast for the eyes. Here nymphs entwine themselves in each others arms whispering sweet phrases into each others ears. Somewhere in the deepest scented roses Venus lies in the arms of Adonis her lover as he tells her the poetry in his heart. Along the pathways a young man in love gives his girl friend a bouquet of roses and they fall into each others arms with delightful kisses. Here in these gardens we are filled with poetry, drunk on sweet scents, and inspired with beauty.

In sacred places roses grow to honour the love we have for the beauty of life and its gift to us. It is always the giving of the rose that expresses this love. Here is the beauty of companionship and the loving relationship that develops and matures. Here our heart strings find their harmonies in others. This love within deep relationships is the very heart and spirit of the rose.

*'If your thought is a rose*
*You are a rose garden.'*

Mevlana Jelalludin Rumi

# SHEPHERD'S PURSE
## *Capsella Bursa-Pastoris*

Shepherd's purse blooms in the early spring and continues to blossom through the summer. It has the most delicate lime green leaves that form a green rosette at the base. The slender stalk slowly grows very finely upwards until the flower heads form. They then burst into small white flowers of simple petals and golden centres. These later form heart shaped seed cases. The slender stem continues to grow upwards producing flowers and then seed cases until there is a whole string of hearts rising to the sky. As the summer dries the purses, they become golden hearts until they are cut back with the field grasses. It is a plant that is found all over the world and its leaves flourish most of the year round. It grows in the poorest of soils maybe only a few inches high, but in rich soil it can grow to a couple of feet. Its odour is like cress and rather forceful. Its taste is sharp and gives cow milk a sharpness when the cows eat the leaves. The seeds themselves are enjoyed by all birds and when chickens are fed on the plant in spring the eggs are of a stronger flavour. The Latin name capsella means a little case or box. When the heart shaped seed cases are opened they break in two and all the seeds fall out. The seed cases are in the shape of purses that the medieval peasants used to carry money. The plant for this reason was nicknamed pickpocket.

When it is dried and made into tea it was considered by herbalists to be one of the best teas for stopping hemorrhages of all kinds and especially bleeding from the kidneys. Culpepper said that it helped bleeding of both internal and external wounds. He also said that if it is bound to the wrists or soles of the feet it will help with jaundice. Poultices can help with inflammation. The ointment was used to help heal all wounds and to aid an earache. It has also been used to treat diarrhoea and dysentery. It was used for bladder ulcers and abscesses. Externally the bruised leaves were used for bruises and sprains.

Today it is used medicinally for helping with hemorrhages of any kind. During the first world war when goldenseal was in short supply, shepherd's purse was used for staunching blood. It is a treatment for heavy uterine bleeding and can be used for any bleeding from nose bleeds to blood in the urine. It is also used for cystitis, dysentery, diarrhoea and eye problems.

The plant is also thought to be anti-inflammatory and can reduce fever.

Imagine having a pocket of wonders. Here when your energy is slow there is a pocket of vitality full of the wisdom of doing those things that are most important first. When you have not enough nourishment, here in this little pocket you find a hidden valley full of growing fruits of all descriptions. When you are not confident about where you are, you look in the pocket and find big boots to step into that enable you to see the vast expanses of heaven and earth filling you with great esteem. Then when all the little things are not right you find that in this pocket there is a storekeeper with just what you need in his little shop. Then again when the load you are carrying seems to be weighing you down, in the pocket you find a boat to carry all your unnecessary cares down the river and far away.

It is in the spring that shepherd's purse sends its flowers upwards towards the sky and creates its heart shaped seed heads. What great treasures lie in these sweet purses that are formed one after the other. Here is the future in all its promise. Here is the hope that comes with each new morning. Here is a pocket that is like a bubbling spring, rushing full of energy to bring a lightness, brightness and hopefulness to what is happening all around. This is the spirit of the shepherd's purse, a fullness of golden hope that gets us over all of life's bumps and difficulties.

*'Mother Earth has worked all winter long in making her dress,*
*beautiful dress, but it is green.*
*About the early spring she adds some wild flowers to it.*
*And whenever she gets ready she drops her skirt*
*down the mountain side,*
*you can see it across the mountain downhill,*
*her skirt is full with all the flowers-all kinds of flowers.*
*That's our Mother's skirt that she had worked on all winter long.'*

Edna Chekelelee

*'If you want to be happy all your life*
*make a garden.'*

Chinese Proverb

# STAR OF BETHLEHEM
## *Ornithogalum Umbellatum*

Star of Bethlehem is an exquisite white flower with delicate fine lines of green on the petals. The leaves are dark green and form the most elegant shapes like velvet ribbons of decoration. The flowers resemble the very stars themselves. They only open in full sunlight and close at dusk to reflower the next morning. When walking through the mountains it is like magic when these tiny stars appear near old oak trees in the striped light of the sunshine streaming through the leaves of the forest. They are like gifts of hope and joy. It is said that they sprang from the tears of Eve as she went from heaven. The flowers themselves are often used as decorations for the altars of the virgin Mary representing her purity and also the time of ascension. They were thought to symbolize devotion and the purity of the heart.

In Roman times the flowers were said to first come from the drops of Juno's celestial milk that fell as the giant Hercules was being suckled at her rosy breasts. The Greek name ornithogalum means bird's milk flower. The Arabs called them dove's dung because they flower in whole fields in the spring and are thought to come from doves and dung because they are dug out of the soil. They have been called the star of Hungary, the lesser Spanish star, and the great Arabische star.

Pilgrims in caravans going to Mecca often carried them to eat as food. The bulbs were eaten raw or boiled with sauces or roasted over the fire like chestnuts. Large quantities of the bulbs were stored in Cairo and Damascus for journeys to Mecca and for food in times of drought. They grow abundantly in the woods near Bath where they were cooked and sold as a vegetable in the market and called Bath asparagus. The juice of the American bulb is used as a tonic to bring back thinning hair.

For Bach the star of Bethlehem was used for shock of any kind and its function was to neutralize that shock. If the shock was neutralized then the recuperation could be accelerated. The shock could be anything from sudden bad news, a fright, or a disappointment. It could be that the person who received the shock may not have noticed anything at the time however later developed a skin disease or nervous disorder or coronary problem. Whether the shock was of the past or a recent disappointment or stress, the star of Bethlehem would help neutralize the effect and help the treatment move forward.

Nature constantly tries to balance herself. When there is a really hot summer the next one may have more rain than normal. When there is little snow in the winter, the spring rains may come more frequently. Seven years of drought are said to bring seven years of plenty. The star of Bethlehem has five petals, one for each season. On one leaf dances the hope of spring, on another the warm heart fires of summer, on another the bounty of the harvest, on still another the inspiration and letting go of autumn and on the last the vitality and resources of water. Contained in the richly nourishing bulb of the star of Bethlehem is the food for all seasons. Here is the rich distribution of the harvest, the great esteem and inspiration of the spring, the palaces of warmth, joy and laughter of the summer sunshine, the rich uniqueness of each individual of the autumn and the vitality of fresh water springs of the winter. The star of Bethlehem has the ability to bring back the order and balance of the seasons. We then have the nourishment of each season that feeds the next so all flows in harmony.

Imagine the rains of winter softening the seed within you and it suddenly coming to life. Then the warm sunshine and earthly nutrients enable your leaves to grow and your flowers to blossom. As the summer ends the seed heads form ready to be harvested or blown to the wind. In autumn these seeds are fed by the compost of fallen leaves and are again nourished by the snows and rains of winter to come alive again in spring. When something has been knocked out of this natural order, it is the star of Bethlehem we can call on to renourish what is needed so the energy of that season can once again enhance life and enable it to flow smoothly.

*'The life of man is a circle from childhood to childhood,*
*and so it is in everything where power moves.'*

Black Elk

*'Bamboo bends before the storm*
*While the pine is broken in two.*
*The difference is the living centre.'*

Lao Tsu

# VALERIAN
## *Valeriana Officinalis*

Valerian grows in some of the most amazing places. She roots in small amounts of soil in the rocks of old walls or along steep banks and grows a pale green stem full of triangular leaves designed to catch water. In the centre grows a long stem with a cluster of pink-red flowers at the top. She brings beauty out of the smallest amount of nourishment and with fine roots gains the most balanced toe hold in the rockiest of places. The flowers have a strong almost almond or vanilla like odour. The root also has a strong odour but more musty. In the middle ages the flowers were used as a perfume and spice and the root was placed among linen and clothes to give them an unusual scent. Rats are attracted to the smell and it is said that the Pied Piper carried it to attract the rats away from Hamelin. The leaves are edible and can be used in salads or fried. The root can be added to soups. The name cetranthus comes from the Greek kentron which means a spur and anthos which means a flower. Valerian either comes from the Latin valere which means to be in health or from the story that Valerius was the first person to use the plant medicinally.

It is said that a girl who wears valerian will never lack for lovers. It is used as a love charm in potions and powders. If a sprig of the plant is pinned to a woman's clothing it is said men will follow her like children. It was also used to help couples from fighting and was hung in the home to protect the house from lightening. It can be placed in pillows to help with falling asleep.

Valerian has been used as a sedative and relaxant since the times of the Greeks for it reduces nervous tension and promotes restful sleep. It has been found in the medicine bags of Native American warriors who used it to heal cuts and wounds. During the middle ages it was called an all heal plant. For this reason it was grown in monastery gardens for its scent as well as calming and pain relieving qualities. It is said that men who begin to fight, if they are given the juice of valerian, will make peace almost immediately. Culpepper said of the Greek valerian that it helps in nervous complaints, headaches and trembling. It also helps with palpitations of the heart, and in hysteric cases. It is said to be a nervine tonic that eases pain and aids sleep and is tranquilizing without having side effects. During the first and second world wars, valerian was used for treating shell shock and nervous stress. The root can be used to treat insomnia, cramp, intestinal colic, period pain and rheumatism. It is also useful for migraine, palpitations, stomach cramps and hysteria. It induces sleep and minimizes stress and strain. A decoction of the root has been used as a facial wash and a soothing bath.

In modern times valerian is used to help relieve stress as it is a safe and non-addictive relaxant that both reduces nervous tension and anxiety as well as promoting restful sleep. It improves sleep quality and lowers blood pressure. Valerian reduces mental over-activity and nervous excitability. It has a calming rather than directly sedative effect on the mind. It relaxes over contracted muscles and is helpful for muscle tensions, asthma, colic, irritable bowel syndrome and menstrual pain. It is also used for tremors, panic sweating and palpitations.

Imagine lying on a soft cloud drifting through the air that is fresh and clear. You look down and see the earth below in ways you have never seen it before. You are no longer caught up in the small details but can see its entire rivers, mountains and cities. Your mind has clearer vision and you become more and more fascinated with each passing view of the earth below. The rivers only exist because of the earth they run through. The forests grow because of both water and the earth. The city is a small part of the wilderness around it. You now have a vision of the great beauty of the earth and how all is connected together. You more clearly see your place in this greatness. Everything becomes a part of everything else and very special in its own way.

Valerian is what dreams are made of. It is like walking up a mountain on a bright clear day and being able to see everything in more detail and in relation to everything else. This clears the mind and helps to make us understanding those things that weigh us down or we can't seem to get beyond. Here we can see life in a new perspective in the same way dreams sometimes rework the events of the day into richer images that can transform themselves in many ways in the night. It is like being at the quiet calm source of our being where our cares and worries can be washed afresh and we can flow more easily with what life brings rather than being caught in what we expect.

*'How long we will have the maple is up to the people.*
*How long we will have the strawberry is up to the people.*
*How long we will have water to survive is up to the people.*
*Every individual can make a difference.'*

Audrey Shenandoah

*'The world is ruled by letting things take their course.*
*It cannot be ruled by interfering.'*

Lao Tsu

# GORSE
## Ulex Europaeus

Gorse flowers are a vibrant yellow colour that bring pure sunshine to the hillsides in the spring. They have strong green coloured leaves and thorns that sheep like to rub their backs on. The flowers are slightly scented with a sweet odour. The bushes grow in rocky places and provide shelter from the wind on high ground. The seed heads burst with a crackling sound in hot weather scattering the seeds all around. The name, gorse comes from the Anglo-Saxon word gorst which refers to the waste-land where it is found. The Latin name ulex was given by Pliny but there seems to be no significance to the word. It is one of the first shrubs to flower providing the bees with rich spring food after the long hard winter. Branches were carried around the herds of sheep to bring good luck to the shepherd.

There is a Devon match making dance using gorse. The men would dance with gorse branches made into a faggot. The girls would then choose a partner. If they then married, the faggot would be used to bake the first loaf of bread in their new home. It is said that when the gorse is blooming the kissing is in season. Often gorse is carried in bridal bouquets for luck. Gorse has long been used as fuel for ovens, cattle feed, as a chimney brush, for colouring Easter eggs and for making gorse and stone hedges. The burnt ash was used to make a solution of lye which mixed with clay made a kind of soap. The buds make a sweet scented tea and the flowers give a beautiful yellow dye. The seeds are nutritious and can be eaten. The sharp spines of the gorse were once used as a comb for cleaning wool. When the flowers are given to a woman they are considered to bring good luck. In Welsh folklore the gorse was believed to be a protection against spirits. Gorse is also said to attract gold.

Gerard says that the seeds can be used for fevers, or jaundice, stones and laxness of the bowels. It is traditionally believed to make one of the best wines and the flowers were once used to flavour whiskey. The tea of the fresh flowers is diuretic. In tea or in the bath the gorse flowers can bring hope and positivity for the depressed. Gorse flower wine was drunk to help bring back the hope of spring.

Bach says of the gorse bush, that it is for those who have lost heart and suffer from hopelessness and despair where after many treatments they are told nothing more can be done for them. It brings back the hope of recovery in long or chronic illnesses. If given at the beginning of a long illness it will give the patient hope of recovery and that is often the first step towards a cure. The patient often looks as if they need sunshine to drive the clouds away. The positive aspect of gorse is found in patients who have a positive faith and hope and are certain in the end they will overcome all difficulties.

Imagine a tree that sits on an unprotected hillside. It is battered and deformed from the winds and weather of the seasons and its growth slowed by the poor nourishment in the soil. And yet despite these conditions it still manages to grow into a tree with its roots in the earth and its branches reaching to the sky. All around the tree then grow gorse bushes full of their spiky branches and warm yellow flowers in spring. Slowly over the years they provide a hedge that protects the tree. It is able to grow straighter and taller and produces more leaves that in turn nourish the soil both for the tree and the gorse bushes. When we have endured for a long time through illness, depression, and feel hunger, loneliness and abandonment, then the spirit of gorse can be a salve for the wounds and hurts we have suffered by giving us a protective shield and sheltered place to recover. Here we can refind the strength and nourishment to grow taller, fuller, and stronger.

*'The patient must be in a certain frame of mind-it must be flexible.*
*He must work in conjunction with the medicine.*
*He must have faith in its power in order to help it.*
*In the Indian philosophy of sickness,*
*it is thought that one's mind must be freed of worry and distrust*
*in order that the patient may get well.'*

Jesse Cornplanter

# ST JOHN'S WORT
## *Hypericum*

St John's Wort has yellow star shaped flowers with bright centres. The flowers are like ornaments of sunshine all over the leafy green plant. It grows in the height of the summer producing one magnificent flower after another. The stem divides into multiple stalks that produce delicate leaves and heads of multiple blooms. The flowers are both delicate and charming with centres full of long golden stamen. It appears where it wants to in the garden with a definite mind of its own. It is the herb of St John whose festival is on the summer solstice. It is a celebration of the changing season where blessings are sought for the crops and the return of the New Year. If the plant at this time was smoked through the sacred fire it was thought its healing qualities would greatly increase. It would then contain the full power of the sun at its height and strength.

St John's wort is said to protect against enchantments and spirits and to frighten witches and goblins with its spicy breath. Its name hypericum comes from the Greek and means over an apparition. It was said that a whiff of its odour would cause evil spirits to fly away. If it is gathered on midsummer it is said to cure melancholy and keep mental illness away. When hung by the window it is thought to protect against thunderbolts, and fire. Placed beneath a pillow it is said to help women dream of their future husbands. When carried it is said to ward off fevers and colds as well as making soldiers invincible.

Medicinally it has been used for chest and lung complaints, bladder troubles, worms, dysentery, haemorrhages, jaundice, children's incontinence at night, hysteria and nervous depression. The oil made with flowers soaked in olive oil is good for burns, cuts and bruises. Culpepper says that a tincture of the flowers put into the spirit of wine helps both melancholy and madness. Outwardly it is used for bruises, wounds and contusions. The seeds in wine are said to help with vomiting and those stung by venomous creatures.

In modern times it is used where there is nerve irritation like in ticklely coughs, neuritis or neuralgia. The ointment is used for wounds, boils, and inflammations as well as ulcers. A tincture is thought to be good for depression. The whole herb is effective against many viral infections. It has long been used by herbalists for anxiety, tension, insomnia, depression and for the menopause. It is also a good tonic for the liver and gallbladder. The red oil made from the flowers steeped in olive oil is an excellent antiseptic used externally for wounds, cramps, burns and nerve pain. It can also be taken internally for peptic ulcers and nerve pain.

There are many times in life when there is no one solution. Times when we seemed to be pulled in many directions at once. This may come at times of crisis when a family member is ill or there has been a divorce or the demands of job are in a different direction to the needs of the family. It could also be that we are trying to move in one direction but the direction of the currents of life are sending us elsewhere. Maybe the demands of being a parent are different to a career. It is when we feel these splits and divisions that St John's wort can help bring back our balance and harmony. It helps us to see that if we deal with what is most important and dearest to us, then the other demands cease to be so demanding and seem to get done in what time is left. Priorities get sorted out and space can come into life again. Otherwise a sense of being overwhelmed takes over and we become like a leaf blown in all directions by the wind or like leaves suddenly scattered by a sudden gust. Here we can listen to our heart and find what is best for those we are close to and choose the work that is dearest to our hearts. This refinding of our centre of balance and the ability to see all directions as a part of the whole is the spirit of St John's wort. All the diverse ways become a part of that whole and we are able to move again from the centre.

*'Then I was standing on the highest mountain of them all,*
*and round about me was the whole hoop of the world.*
*And while I stood there I saw more than I can tell*
*and I understood more than I was,*
*for I was seeing in a sacred manner*
*the shapes of all things in the spirit,*
*and the shape of all shapes as they must live together like one being.*
*And I saw that the sacred hoop of my people was*
*one of many hoops that made one circle.'*

Black Elk

# HEMP AGRIMONY
## *Eupatorium Cannabinum*

Hemp agrimony grows in later summer. Its tall central stalk, similar in colour to rhubarb, is full of rich green leaves and at the top are flowers of a delicate peachy pink. It is one of the tall giants of the garden. The name Eupatoria is thought to come from the King Mithridates Eupator VI who lived in the first century BC. He was famous for his snake bite concoction that was also used for other infections. This Mithridate confection as it was called was only withdrawn from the London Pharmacopoeia in 1746. Argemone was a word given to plants by the Greeks for those plants which healed the eyes. The common name Joe Pye Weed was given to the plant because a Native American called Joe Pye used the plant in the treatment of typhus.

In the middle ages it was used for skin problems, scurvy and jaundice. It has been used to purify the blood and for arthritis and rheumatism. Tinctures and tea were given for influenza or a feverish chill. Country folks used the leaves as a wound herb, purgative and to lay on bread to keep it from moulding. Today it is used as a detoxifying herb for fevers, colds, flu, and other acute viral conditions. It simulates the waste removal in the kidneys. The root can be used as a laxative. The whole plant is considered to be a tonic. It helps to maintain resistance to acute viral and other infections. It is said by carrying a leaf one can attract love. It is also used in group rituals to bring the group spirit together.

Hemp agrimony has a fullness that vibrates all the flowers around it. It is not a plant for comfort but shakes our very foundations and opens up new pathways and ways of sensitivity. When the spirit has been closed, hidden, and covered over, this plant can bring back contact with our deep inner core. Here we can move through the pain and discomfort of past difficulties and what has happened can be addressed and changed. Hemp agrimony is a candle producing a glimmer of light in the dark nights and passageways of life. Here we can find the understanding and compassion to move forward, to forgive, to understand and to refind the inner strength and contact with the heart. Here the heart can feel the emotions of life in all their strength, and beauties. From these depths our compassion can give us the means of helping others.

# BUTTERCUP
## *Ranunculacea Aeris*

Buttercups are the brightest and most friendliest flower ever to be found. To see a field of buttercups waving their sweet smiles of rich yellow is to feel as if friends are all around. To lie in a field of buttercups is like being surrounded by hundreds of bright warm hearts full of gracious sunshine. Buttercups simply makes the heart feel full of warmth and companionship. The leaves are variated and rich green like hands reaching out to touch every experience around it. The cups of yellow that form the flowers are a bright shiny yellow and full of pollen dust that cover the hungry insects busily drinking the nectar. Buttercups delightfully wave and dance wherever they are. The Latin name refers to the bulb like swelling of its root and one of the popular names was St Anthony's turnip. In France it is called jaunet from the brilliance of its blossoms. It has also been called frog's foot from the shape and colour of its leaves, and golden cup from the flowers. The roots have been boiled and eaten with various sauces. Wild pigs are particularly fond of the roots.

The roots have the property of inflaming and blistering the skin. It has been used to treat the joints in this way especially in gout. In the middle ages beggars would sometimes use it to open sores to gain sympathy. It is said the juice placed in the nostrils causes sneezing and can cure some kinds of headaches. It has also been used to help with rheumatism as a poultice. A tincture made with wine is said to cure shingles and help with sciatica. Culpepper says that he never saw anything yellower. He says never to use it internally but the leaves can be used to draw a blister. The common field buttercup leaves can be used to remove warts. A homeopathic tincture has also been used as a remedy for irritating skin conditions as eczema and rheumatic complaints. The plant is considered toxic and is not used in herbalism today.

Imagine suddenly having contact with all your friends who you have not seen for a long time. You all meet together over a meal and talk about the things that are important. You laugh together and warmly share what is in your heart and what your hopes and aspirations are. It is this contact that buttercup helps to recreate for a person, putting them back in touch with those who are really dear to them and with whom they can share the most tender feelings.

# ELDER
## Sambucus Nigra

Elder flowers are like lace woven by heavenly hands. They hang from green branches full of large deep green leaves. The whole tree gives a wonderful shade. It is like being in an ancient space of old furnishing and fairy gardens. The odour is strong and pungent and fills the air with strength and dreaminess. The name Elder comes from the Anglo-Saxon word aeld meaning fire. The hollowed elder branches were used in those times to kindle fires by blowing through the hollow centres to give the flame more oxygen. The Latin name sambucus comes from the musical instrument called sambucu. This was a stringed instrument made from the hard wood of the tree. Pan pipes were made in both Greek and Roman times from the branches. It was one of their sacred trees. The elder tree was thought to be the mother of the elves who lived under her roots. It is said to be a dwelling place of good house spirits. Offerings were often left for the tree when asking for her blessings. If any wood from the tree was used the tree was always asked first. It was thought bad luck to burn elder branches unless an offering was left for the tree.

The Druids gathered the last berries that rested on the elder trees in December and would make them into a strong wine to initiate clairvoyance. The green branches were buried with the dead in British long barrows to protect them on their journey to the otherworld. It has long been a tree of protection and when planted near a house is said to protect it from lightening and to keep bad spirits away. If a stick is worn it wards off attackers of any kind. A stick of elderberry was carried at weddings for good luck. A love charm could be made by putting the flowers into ale or wine which if shared with a loved one meant marriage within a year. To bless a person or place, the leaves and berries should be scattered to the four winds naming what is to be blessed. Pregnant women would kiss the tree for good fortune for the coming baby. Elderberries placed under a pillow allow peaceful sleep. Warts are said to be cured by rubbing them with a green elder twig and then burying the twig. Rheumatism is said to be helped by carrying a knotted twig in the pocket. Magicians have used its wood for centuries to make magic wands.

Its wood is white and finely grained and has been used for musical instruments, needles, weaving nets, combs, and small toys. The bruised leaves placed on a hat is said to prevent flies from settling because of its strong smell. An infusion of the leaves dabbed on the skin is said to keep mosquitoes away. The rich deep purple coloured berries are made into cordials, wines and preserves. The wine was used to help with rheumatic pain especially if mixed with port. The whole tree is thought to promote long life.

Elder has been called the medicine chest of the country people. Even the fungus that grows on the tree is eatable and was used for throat and mouth inflammations. In the middle ages virtually every ailment of the body could be cured by the tree from the plague to toothache. The leaves were used externally as an ointment for bruises, sprains, and wounds and could also be used for piles if mixed with camphor and lard. Elder flower water was used as an eye and skin lotion. It was also used for clearing the complexion of freckles and sunburn. Teas of the flowers were used for bronchial and pulmonary infections, fevers, measles, flu and influenza. Externally elder flowers have been used to ease pain and inflammation of the joints. The flowers placed in oil is a remedy for wounds, burns and scalds. The berries are used in many ways being full of vitamins. They are made into a full bodied wine which when drunk hot is said to be a good preventative against influenza and chills. Tea made from the berries is good for colic and diarrhoea. Culpepper says that the young leaves boiled up are good for phlegm and choler. He goes on to say that the bark can be used as a purgative and for the dropsy. The wine he used for bringing on a woman's courses and to provoke urine.

Current day uses of the flowering tops include infusions for coughs, colds and flu. The infusion is relaxing and helps to reduce fever. Infusions can also be used for chronic congestion, allergies, ear infections and candidiasis. If taken before the hay fever season they can reduce the severity of hay fever attacks. They also promote sweating and urine production and can be helpful for arthritic conditions. The berries are rich in vitamin C.

In Buddhism there is a ceremony for when there are differences among members of the community and is described by Thich Nhat Hanh as laying down the straw to cover muddy ground. Muddy ground is not pleasant to walk on so paths are laid in order that we can walk through the woods and fields without sinking in the mud. In this ritual, the elders of the community are invited to resolve the conflict. Everyone simply listens to the wise ones who often say something like, 'We are all brothers and sisters of the same family and we have to forgive each other. We have to put straw down on the muddy path so that we can walk together'. They then propose a general amnesty and everyone in conflict bows before the wise ones and forgets the conflict. Somehow when someone speaks with such great wisdom, the compassion in everyone is touched and everyone again can accept each other and the peace that results. Elder is used to call on the ancestors. Here the elders meet to help bring the great conflicts within someone into peace and harmony. Here we can find the wisdom of all generations of wise people who have gone before to help with the disorder and disharmony that is going on within the person. They come and simply lay straw on the path so the person no longer has to walk in the mud and can find their feet again.

> *'As we listen in the wind,*
> *we can hear the sounds and songs of our ancestors,*
> *and as we walk on the ground,*
> *we are walking on the faces of those yet unborn.*
> *Let us make a beautiful dream, full of hope, clean water,*
> *good land, and a good way of life for them.'*

Winona LaDuke

# VERVAIN
## *Verbena Officinalis*

Vervain is delicate, fine, and almost a spirit whisper of the garden whose charms of protection have been revered for centuries. Her tiny blue flowers come out in late summer gathering the changing sunshine of the shortening days. They come out one by one growing at the end of long stems and are like constellations of stars suspended on green. Her leaves are crafted like fine fingers balancing the plant in perfect proportions. The tiny delicate leaves are like minute glimmers and reflections of inspiration. The plant is hardly visible but when seen inspires the heart and very vision of what is hidden in nature. It opens the doors of enchantment. The common name of vervain comes from the Celtic word ferfaen which means to drive away the stone. It meant it could drive away emotional pressures.

The Romans believed that if a room were sprinkled with water of vervain all the guests would be merrier. Both the Greeks and Romans held the belief that the plant was sacred to the goddess of love. The ancient Egyptians believed that the plant was formed from the tears of the Goddess Isis. Because of this it was a major ingredient of love potions. The Romans called it herba sacra and used it to cleanse temples and to place on altars during ceremonies. Both the Romans and Celts would carry the plant into battle for protection. It has been used as herb of sacred rites and protection with the Romans, Celts, Hebrews, Egyptians, Greeks, and Persians. The Persian magicians greeted the rising sun holding vervain in their hands. The Pawnee Indians used it to enhance their dreams.

It was one of the plants put into the Cauldron of Cerridwen of the Celts which was said to bestow the powers of eloquence, inspiration, prophecy and song on initiates. It is said that the goddess Cerridwen made a potion for her son Afgddu (Utter Darkness) that would contain all the wisdom of the three realms. She collected the herbs and brewed them in a cauldron for a year and a day. A little boy, Gwion fed the fire. One day three drops fell on his finger and he licked them off to ease the pain. Suddenly he could see all things and was at one with all the world past, present and future. He became the great bard and seer Taliesin. Vervain since those times has been used as a herb that is sacred to poets and singers. It is said its spirit can enable a person to see like the giant hawk from a great height and perspective. It is a plant used at Samhain in the autumn to protect the seeds asleep in the ground with the wisdom of the ancestors honoured at that time of year.

Vervain so likes man that it only grows within a mile of human habitation. A piece of vervain hung over the door is said to prevent nightmares. It was often buried in fields to help with a good harvest. Hanging it in the home is said to protect against bad spirits, lightening and storms. It was believed that if a bride picked a sprig on the wedding morning, then the marriage would have love and faithfulness. It is believed that if the dried herb is scattered around the home it is a peace bringer and can be worn to calm the emotions. If the herb is buried in the garden wealth is said to flow and plants will thrive. It can also bring youth and if its juice is placed on the body it can cure disease and guard future health. If someone you know has taken something from you then if you wear vervain and confront the person you will regain the possession. If vervain is placed in a baby's cradle the child will grow up happy and have a love of learning. When the juice of vervain is placed on the body, the person is able to see the future, have wishes fulfilled, attract lovers and be protected.

Medicinally its infusion has been used to help digestion and as a sedative for sleep. It has been taken to de-toxify the body, promote urine and as a tonic for nervous exhaustion, relieving stress and tension. It can be used as a gargle for infections and swellings of the mouth and throat. Externally it can be applied for rheumatism, bruises, cuts, burns and sprains. Bruised leaves were worn around the neck for headaches and to guard against snake-bite. Culpepper said that it could help with swelling of the private parts. He also said that it opens obstructions and is cleansing and healing for jaundice, the dropsy and the gout. It also helps with diseases of the stomach, liver and spleen.

Bach found vervain to be a remedy for the extremes of mental energy which manifests in over effort, stress and tension. He said vervain people hold strong views. They maybe so high strung and fret and fuss that they can not do all they want to do. They seem never able to relax their mind or body and this produces a great strain and tiredness. They have the enthusiasm and the excitement of the possession of great knowledge and the burning desire to bring all to the same state, but their enthusiasm may hinder their cause. The positive side is seen in the wise calm man who knows his own mind and who accepts the opinion of others. Here is a fluid mind always ready to listen to others and able to change its opinions.

Today vervain is used as a remedy for coughs, colds and diarrhoea. It can be used as a tonic for digestion to improve food absorption. It is used as a restorative for the nervous system as it has a mild antidepressant action and can be used to treat anxiety and nervous exhaustion following long term stress, or for people with chronic illness. It can also alleviate headaches. It is given for jaundice, gallstones, asthma, insomnia, premenstrual tension and fevers as well as helping labour contractions and breast milk production.

When we are born the stars line up in a special order to welcome our birth. They are our special combination of strengths, weaknesses, gifts and destinies. At the moment of birth, the stars overhead send their blessing down honouring the uniqueness of each child. As we grow these shining lights in the dark sky remain a constant gift of wonder and inspiration. We can watch as the constellations change throughout the seasons and know that all emotions will blossom and whither and change as life continually progresses. Vervain is like a storehouse of night stars giving us what we need to nourish our spirit through its journey so that we too may shine in the dark and move easily in the constantly changing constellations of life.

*'They spoke no words*
*The visitor, the host and the flower.'*

Japanese Poem

# CAMPION
## *Silene Latifolia*

Campion is full of delicate Japanese lanterns decorated with sweet white flower petals. The stalks grow in segmented sections in all directions with soft long fingered leaves of blue-green. Its name comes from the 14th century word for champion and the flowers were made into garlands for tournaments. The name also comes from the French word compagne meaning an open countryside where the plant grows in the wild. The shoots can be eaten as vegetables either sauteed or boiled with various sauces. It was also called the herb of thunder and was thought to protect against storms. Gerard thought it was good against snake bite. It is not a plant used in modern herbalism.

Campion helps when there is a need for growth. It is for when someone does not have the courage to move forward, or has been too often disappointed. They maybe frightened or have been hurt too much or have been ill for a long time and no longer have the ability to grow and mature. Campion can then come along and be their champion, their friend and a person to walk with so the person can begin to take new steps at first with help and then on their own. The plant wraps its abundance of leaves around the person and encourages them to grow and develop. Here the shyness grows into wonder, the hurt becomes compassion and understanding, the fear becomes delight, and the sadness becomes strength.

*'The clearest sign of grace is that from dung come flowers,*
*from the bulbous sludge, buds and then sweet pears.*
*The ground's generosity takes in our compost and grows beauty!*
*Try to be more like the ground.*
*Give back better, as a rough clod returns an ear of corn,*
*a tassel, a barley awn, this sleek handful of oats.'*

Mevlana Jalluddin Rumi

# BIRTHWORT
## *Aristolochia Clematitis*

Birthwort is almost primordial. The first flower on earth was the arum with heart shaped leaves and a single stem flower in the middle. The birthwort is smaller but has the same heart shaped leaves and a bright yellow half moon for a flower. It is like a flower of prehistoric times surrounded by fern coloured leaves. The seedheads that form are pear shaped and full of seeds. It grows in most soils and flowers in the height of the summer. Its root is long and shaped like a spindle. The plant like the arum, has an odour that attracts flies in particular, and is like rotting meat. The Latin name arstolochia means best birth which may come from its use at birth to speed up labour and help with the expelling of the afterbirth and infection. It also comes from the flower itself which resembles the womb and birth canal. Pliny suggested that if a woman wanted a son then she should use birthwort and the flesh of an ox in sacrifice. The plant was often found in monastic gardens and was believed to be effective against the evil eye and also for snake bites. It is sometimes used in incense after the birth of a child to thank the Goddess for a safe birth or to help at the inception of creative projects.

Theophrastus of the second century BC says that the plant was used to treat disorders of the uterus, reptile bites and sores on the head. The Native Americans used it to treat snake bite, stomachache, toothache, and fevers. The plant is poisonous if used internally. The flowering stems have been used externally for centuries as a stimulant in gout and rheumatism, for fevers, neuralgia, and for removing obstructions. It has also been used to speed up labour, to dispel the afterbirth and as a dangerous solution for abortion. A decoction used externally can also be used for eczema, wounds, ulcers and other skin complaints.

It is not in use very much today, and is considered poisonous if taken internally. But it was formerly used to treat wounds, sores and snake bite. The fresh juice was traditionally applied to induce labour. It has been used after child birth to prevent infection and as a potent menstruation inducing drug and dangerous abortifacient. A decoction was applied to heal ulcers and for asthma and bronchitis. Chinese research has shown it to be effective as a wound healer but until its safety has been cleared in Europe it should not be used medicinally.

Family relationships are never perfect and birthwort helps when there are difficulties between mother and daughter or father and son or any other combination of family divisions and strifes. It enables the person to calm their own reaction to what has happened and to see the other persons viewpoint. It is like a grandmother suddenly arriving with a cake. She has everyone sit down for tea to share a good moment rather than staying with the arguments and struggles. This offers a time for each person in the family to see each other family member in their fullness. The difficulties then seem more distant and everyone can bring their needs and strengths to helping each other rather than remaining with the conflict. When one person changes and is able to see the value of the other person then everyone benefits. By changing one energy, all the energy around also changes. These changes are in the spirit of birthwort.

*'Every part of the earth is sacred, every shining pine needle,*
*every sandy shore, every light mist in the dark forest,*
*every clearing, and every winged creature is sacred to my people.*
*We are part of the earth and it is part of us.*
*The fragrant flowers are our sisters,*
*the deer and mighty eagle are our brothers;*
*the rocky peak, the fertile meadows, all things are connected like*
*the blood that unites a family.'*

Chief Seattle

# FLAX
## *Linum Perenne*

Flax is the richest of blue flowers, on the most slender and delicate stem full of tiny green fingered leaves. It lights up the whole field with deep blue gem droplets. Each flower petal is beautifully lined in exquisite detail leading the most wayward of insects to its golden nectared centre. It is fine and refined like the very linen it produces. Here is pure strength in the most delicate of stems able to withstand strong winds with its flexibility and graciousness. Its name linum comes from its use as threads that are woven into the making of linen.

It was thought that the goddess Arachne, who was in the form of a spider, first taught the Greeks how to weave cloth. This cloth made from flax was used by Odysseus for his sails, fish nets, threads, ropes, string and clothes. This fine linen is mentioned in the Bible as well. The seeds and linen woven from the plant have been found in the tombs of the Egyptians. It was the German goddess Hulda who was thought to have shown the Germans how to weave the cloth from the plant. It is the sacred plant of weavers and sewers. The weaver goddess is thought to weave the web of life and to intertwine the warps and wefts of fate. She is said to generate the net of the cosmos. The seeds were thought to protect the home and if placed in a wallet or money box would attract good fortune. Placing a bit of flax on shoes is said to ward off poverty. The seeds have been eaten in times of famine and have been added to breads since ancient times. It is said if children dance in a field of flax when they are seven then they will receive the gift of beauty.

Pliny said that linseed could be applied to all forms of active life. For him it was a great marvel of the earth. Culpepper says it is of great use against inflammations, tumours and imposthumes. He goes on to say that the oil is good for the diseases of the lungs and chest. It also helps the colic and the stone. The oil extracted from the seed is known as linseed oil and has for centuries been used to treat tonsillitis, sore throats, coughs, colds, and constipation. It can be mixed with lime water and used for scalds, burns, and sunburn. Infusions are used for the treatment of catarrh, bronchitis, urinary infections and pulmonary infections. Externally it has been used for boils, ulcers, cuts, and inflammations. An infusion of the seeds can be given for inflammatory bowel disease and cystitis.

In modern times flax has been shown to be rich in unsaturated fats and a valuable remedy for many intestinal problems and chest problems. The seed taken whole can soothe irritation throughout the digestive tract and can act as a mild laxative. External poultices of crushed seeds may be useful in treating chronic coughs, brochitis, pleurisy and emphysema. A poultice may also be applied to relieve painful boils. Linseed oil mixed with red wine has been used as a wound healer. The mature seeds are used as the immature seeds may be toxic to some extent

Here the strands of our life can be woven together in a great tapestry. We can begin to see how each step enriches the next and where the strongest threads lie. When we need to reflect in order to see more clearly who we are and where we can be going it is this plant that gives us the vision and pride of who we are. Here we can cut through what is distracting and find the openness that sparkles life with just being who we really are. And so like flax we become a delicate but strong crystal blue gem of life sparkling with our special gifts.

*'A walnut kernel shaken against its shell makes a delicate sound,*
*but the walnut taste and sweet oil inside makes unstruck music.*
*Mystics call the shell rattling talk,*
*the other, the taste of silence,*
*or the quiet seclusion where soul sweetens and thrives.'*

Mevlana Jalaluddin Rumi

*'We are all flowers in the Great Spirit's Garden.*
*We share a common root, and the root is Mother Earth.*
*The garden is beautiful because it has different colours in it,*
*And those colours are different traditions and backgrounds.'*

Hopi Grandfather David Monongye

YOUR ANIMAL FRIEND

# JOURNEYING TO PLANT SPIRITS

To journey imaginatively to a plant is as easy as closing your eyes and daydreaming about the plant. Deep in the blue mountains there is an ancient garden where all the flowers still live as magical beings. The animals that live there speak their own languages and yours. The rivers and lakes sing ancient songs. The winds are able to whisper the future. Here the spirit of life shows itself in every living thing. Visiting there is as easy as closing your eyes. Each time you visit this wonderful place the journey maybe different. It may come as a new road, a special path, a strange river boat or a wonderful flight on a bird's wings. There are many ways to find your way there and each is a special and joyful voyage. It is good to take some friends along to help you on the way. They will be able to show you the beauties of the gardens for they have been there before and know the territory well. They will be able to act as a guide for your journey. You must always bring something as a present to give to the wonderful spirits you will meet. You must also remember to thank your guides. The magical beings like gifts and must always be thanked for their help. They will then always be there for you in a special way.

In ancient times everyone knew who their animal friend was. Animals lived everywhere for there were no cities. It was normal to know which animal was your special helper and guide. To find your animal you need to imagine yourself going down into the ground through a magnificent stone archway. Wander down until you see animals all around. Ask the animals that come to you whether or not they are your animal guide. When you find your animal talk to it and ask it what questions you want to know. Share with this friend what you have brought and thank them for being there for you. Tell him you will come back soon and take him to the magic gardens. Tell him goodbye and return the way you came. Now open your eyes and write about or draw your animal guide on the opposite page.

YOUR FRIENDLY GUIDE

We now need to journey to our spirit guide who lives high up in the heaven above us. Close your eyes again and start to climb upwards. You may go up a tree or a mountain or a ladder or fly on a bird. Somewhere you will find a doorway that could be any design imaginable. Knock on the door and wait for someone to invite you in. Tell them you have come to find your guide. It may be your guide himself or herself or the person may take you to your guide. Your guide could be anyone, big or little or funny or serious, or new or ancient. Whoever it is offer them something from your pocket and ask them any questions. They may offer to tell you a story or take you on a journey to show you something or you may just have tea and cakes together. Spend sometime exploring the upper world with your guide and then thank them for the visit and climb down into the world again the same way you came. Draw or write about your guide on the page opposite.

THE GREEN MAN AND YOUR MEDICINE BAG

Now you are ready to journey to the magic gardens deep in the blue mountains. Close your eyes and invite your animal guide and your spirit guide to come with you. You will journey in some special way to the magic garden by walking or taking a boat or by some other means. At the entry to the garden you will see the green man. He will ask you for something and when you have given it to him he will let you pass into the gardens. He will give you something to help you on your way as well as a medicine bag to keep all the wonderful medicines you will find from the plants in the gardens. Explore the gardens and gather magic things to place in your medicine bag. Return with your guides and thank them for helping you. Open your eyes and draw or write about your visit.

The willow tree lives by the lake in the garden. Take your guides to visit her. She is the first tree to flower and brings the springtime. The bees love her catkins because they have a rich syrup nectar that they make into honey. Go and sit with your back to the willow tree and watch how the leaves sparkle with sunlight. Dance with her branches and listen to her singing. She will brighten your spirit and give you a wish for the next year. Ask her to show you her medicine and when you understand thank her and come back the way you came thanking your guides at the end. Draw or write about the willow spirit.

WILLOW

The nettle lives in a rocky part of the garden. Again take your guides to visit her. She is full of fire and will sting you if you touch her. She is the summer sunshine with all its warmth and vitality and joy. She loves to laugh and gives everyone her warmth and joyful sunshine. Take her hand and go with her through the gardens. Ask her for her medicine and thank her for her time. Return with your guides and thank them again for showing you the spirit of nettle. Now draw or write about her spirit.

NETTLE

Now take your guides to visit evening primrose who live right in the centre of the gardens. She is full of rich yellow flowers. Here is everything that is harvested. It is she who helps cut flowers, apples, lavender, cherries and all the vegetables and grains that grow through the summer. When all is ripe she takes her basket and fills it to nourish all life through the winter months to come. Close your eyes and be fed by her spirit and again ask her about her healing powers. When she has fed you with her riches thank her and return with your guides again thanking them before you open your eyes. Again draw or write about the spirit of evening primrose.

EVENING PRIMROSE

Next take your guides to visit plantain. Plantain is an ancient wild grass. It has watched the heavenly changes in the skies for thousands of years. It will show you the beauty of the world and the specialness of all things. Close your eyes and visit its spirit and ask it to show you its medicine. It will also give you something precious to keep. Go with it and explore the heavens and then come back to the garden and thank it for its time. Return with your guides thanking them and then open your eyes and write about or draw plantain.

PLANTAIN

Once again go with your guides to the garden and this time ask them to take you to the spirit of horsetail. Horsetail loves water and its spirit is like looking into a clear pool where you can see your reflection as well as the reflection of the sky over head and the bottom of the pool. Here is a quiet place inside where we can forget our troubles. Plunge into horsetail's refreshing waters and have a swim. Then go for a journey with horsetail and ask her to tell you about her medicine. Thank her for her help and return with your guides to this world again thanking them for their help. Write and draw about horsetail afterwards.

HORSETAIL

These are the five plants of the five seasons. You can journey to any of the other plants in this book is a similar way and then use their medicine in your own special form of healing. You can return anytime to the beautiful gardens and the plant spirits with your guides to help you on the journey. Be sure and thank them and give them anything they may want and remember to give the green man something to help nourish the gardens. Always remember to thank your guides for their help and protection. In this way the gardens will always be there for you.

# BIBLIOGRAPHY

BARKS, Coleman, *The Soul of Rumi,* Harper San Francisco 2001

BARNARD, Julian, *Bach Flower Remedies, Form and Function,*
    Flower Remedy Programme 2002

BARTRAM, T., *Encyclopedia of Herbal Medicine,* British Herbal Medicine
    Association 1995

BASHO, (trans. Stryk, L.), *On Love and Barley, Haiku of Basho,*
    Penguin Books, 1985

BEINFIELD, H. AND KORNGOLD, E., *Between Heaven and Earth:
    A Guide to Chinese Medicine,* Ballentine Books 1991

BLAMEY, M. and GREY-WILSON, C., *The Illustrated Flora of Britain and
    Northern Europe,* Hodder and Stoughton 1989

BOYER, Marie-France, *Tree-Talk, Memories, Myths & Timeless Customs,*
    Thames and Hudson 1996

BREMNESS. L., *Herbs,* Dorling Kindersley Ltd. 1994

BRIERS, Richard, *A Little Light Weeding,* Robson Books 1999

BROWN, Deni, *The Royal Horticultural Society Encyclopedia of Herbs and
    Their Uses,* Dorling Kindersley Ltd. 1995

BRUGES, James, *The Little Earth Book,* Alastair Sawday Publishing 2000

CHANCELLOR, Philip, *Bach Flower Remedies,*
    C.W. Daniel Company Limited 1971

CHEVALLIER, Andrew, *The Encyclopedia of Medicinal Plants,*
    Dorling Kindersley Ltd. 1995

CHOPRA, D., *Perfect Health,* Harmony Books 1991

COWAN, Eliot, *Plant Spirit Medicine,* Swan Raven & Co. 1995

CUCHE, Pierre, *Plantes Du Midi,* Edisud 1999

CUNNINGHAM, Scott, *Cunningham's Encyclopedia of Magical Herbs,*
    Llewellyn Publications 2003

CULPEPER, Nicholas, *The Complete Herbal,* 1649, & *Culpeper's Colour
    Herbal,* Foulsham 1996

EXLEY, Helen, *Garden Lovers Quotations,* Exley, 1992

FRANKLIN, A. and LAVENDER, S., *Herb Craft,*
    Capall Bann Publishing 1996

GERARD, John, *The Herbal,* Dover Publications, Inc. 1975

GRAVES, Robert, *The Greek Myths,* Penguin Books Ltd. 1955
GRIEVE, Mrs. M., *A Modern Herbal,* Dover Publications, Inc. 1971
GRIGSON, Geoffrey, *The Englishman's Flora,* Helicon 1996
GUNTHER, R., *The Greek Herbal of Dioscorides,*
   Oxford University Press 1934
HAAS, Elsom, *Staying Healthy With The Seasons,* Celetial Arts 1981
HAGENEDER, Fred, *The Spirit of Trees, Science, Symbiosis & Inspiration,*
   Floris Books 2000
HOBHOUSE, Penelope, *The Country Gardener,* Frances Lincoln 1989
HOFFMANN, David, *The New Holistic Herbal,* Element 1990
HUXLEY, Anthony, *Creating a Wild Flower Garden,*
   Webb & Bower Ltd 1986
KAVASCH, E. Barrie, *The Medicine Wheel Garden,* Bantam Books 2002
HELMINSKI, Camille and Kabir, *Rumi Daylight,* Threshold 1994
HELMINSKI, Kabir, *The Rumi Collection,* Threshold 1998
K'EOGH, J., *An Irish Herbal,* (ed. Scott, M.), Aquarian Press 1986
LAO TSU, *Tao Te Ching,* (trans. Gia-Fu Feng), Wildwood House Ltd. 1973
KELLAWAY, Deborah, *Women Gardeners,* Virago Press 1995
MABEY, Richard, *Flora Britannica,* Sinclair-Stevenson 1996
McVICAR, Jekka, *Plantes Medicinales,* Editions France Loisirs 1994
MINTER, Sue, *The Healing Garden,* Headline 1995
MOORE, Michael, *Medicinal Plants of the Pacific West,*
   Red Crane Books 1993
MURRAY, M. AND PIZZORNO, J., *Encyclopedia of Natural Medicine,*
   Prima Publishing 1991
ODY, P., *The Complete Medicinal Herbal,* Dorling Kindersley, Ltd. 1993
PAKENHAM, Thomas, *Meetings with Remarkable Trees,*
   Phoenix Illustrated 1996
PENN, Helen, *An Englishwoman's Garden,* BBC Books 1993
PICKLES, Sheila, *The Language of Flowers,* Penhaligons 1989
PLINY THE ELDER, *Natural History,* Penguin Books Ltd. 1991
PODLECH, Dieter, *Herbs and Healing Plants of Britain and Europe,*
   Harper Collins 1996
RENAUX, Alain, *Le Savoir En Herbe,* Les Presses du Languedoc 1998
ROBERT, Suzanne, *Les Plantes de Santé,* Les Presses du Languedoc, 1990

SACKVILLE-WEST, Vita, *Some Flowers,* Pavilion Books Limited 1996

SVOBODA, R., *Ayurveda: Life, Health and Longevity,* Arkana 1992

THE METROPOLITAIN MUSEUM OF ART, *Perennial Pleasures,*
      Crown Publishers, Inc. 1993

THICH NHAT HANH, J*oyfully Together, the Art of Building a
      Harmonious Community*, Parallax Press 2003

THOMS VITALE, Alice, *Leaves in Myth, Magic and Medicine,*
      Stewart, Tabori and Chang 1997

TISSERD, Robert, *The Art of Aromatherapy,* C.W. Daniel Co. Ltd. 1996

TOBYN, Graeme, *Culpeper's Medicine, A Practice of Western Holistic Medicine*
      Element 1997

TODD, Pamela, *Forget-Me-Not, A Floral Treasury,*
      Little Brown and Co. 1993

VOGEL, V., *American Indian Medicine,* University of Oklahoma Press 1970

WARING, Philippa, *The Feng Shui of Gardening,* Souvenir Press 1998

WEEKS, Nora & BULLEN, Victor, *The Bach Flower Remedies,*
      C.W. Daniels Company Ltd. 1964

WEINER, M., *Weiner's Herbal,* Quantum Books 1990

WELLS, Diana, *100 Flowers & How They Got Their Names*, Past Times 1997

WHEELWRIGHT, Edith Grey, *Medicinal Plants and Their History,*
      Dover Publications Inc. 1974

WORSLEY, J.R., *Classical Five-Element Acupuncture Vol. 3,
      The Five Elements and The Officials,* J.R. & J.B. Worsley 1998